THE RACKHEATH AGGIES

📞 01603 773114 *Website:* studentccnac.sharepoint.com/sites/ccnlibraries
email: lis@ccn.ac.uk 🐦 @CCN_Library 📷 ccnlibrary

21 DAY LOAN ITEM

Please return <u>on or before</u> the last date stamped above

A fine will be charged for overdue items

CITY
COLLEGE
NORWICH

D1492784

Colonel Albert J. Shower

THE

RACKHEATH AGGIES

A Tribute to the
467th Heavy Bombardment Group
American Eighth Air Force

DAVID H. KIBBLE-WHITE

THE ERSKINE PRESS
2001

THE RACKHEATH AGGIES

First published in 2001 by
The Erskine Press, The Old Bakery, Banham, Norwich,
Norfolk NR16 2HW

ISBN 1 85297 067 7

British Library Cataloguing-in-Publication Data
A catalogue record of this book is available
from the British Library

Typeset by Waveney Typesetters, Wymondham, Norfolk
Printed by ColourBooks Ltd. Dublin 13, Ireland

ACKNOWLEDGEMENTS

When I began writing this book, I thought it would be easy. I had got what I thought to be all the information – the idea was clear in my mind. How very wrong I was. I had no idea how many people would be involved in one form or another to make it all happen. For this reason I will mention a few names here and thank them for their invaluable help. I am sure I will miss out some, mainly because there are so many and it's difficult to remember them all. So if I have missed out your name, I am sorry, but it does not detract from the very valuable help you have given me.

First I have to say thank you to Terry Reid. If it was not for his nagging, I would not have started on this crazy episode. Also thanks to Martin Davis, my tutor at Norwich City College. Without his help and encouragement this would not have progressed to a book. To Roy and Joan Williams without whom I would have given up long ago. To Kenton White at Redhead Graphics and Design for his reconstruction of the B-24 Liberator and to Zoe and George Christmas for acting as unpaid editors when I became word blind.

To the men of the 467th of course, namely Paul Kuchinski for all his information and encouragement when the going got tough; Rufus and Eunice Webb; Rufus for his memories and photographs and Eunice for jogging his grey matter and sending the information; Colonel Fred Holdrege who not only gave his memories but who corrected me in no uncertain manner when I got it wrong, and to all the other men of the 467th who gave me various snippets or confirmed or denied information that I had. I must mention also Ralph Elliot and his book *Letters Home* and Philip Day's *The Saga of a Reluctant Co-pilot*; both journals helped to confirm several stories and gave me one or two new ones.

This book could not have been written without the help of the people of Rackheath and the surrounding area: Perry Watts, Eric Fiddy, Peter Smith, Ted Jermy, Anthony Gibbs, Trevor Wyborow, Freida Porter, Brenda Ray, Joy Wild, Ken Herbert, Joan Chapman, Mr Basey and many, many more. To all those people I say a big thank you. I must also say a thank you to Martin Bowman, a well respected author of many books dealing with aviation; without his advice, I would have been lost.

[5]

Last, but by no means least, I must mention my wife Meg. She took the brunt of everything; the loneliness when I spent my time wandering off to interview various people; the hours I spent writing and having to listen to this story as it unfolded as I repeatedly tried to get it right; having to do all the work around the house and garden because I was too busy; to my mood swings when I could not get things right. All in all she has been the driving force behind me. Many times I was going to give up but she persuaded me to go on. To her I say the biggest thank you of all.

To everyone involved in putting this book together, be it information, support, encouragement, whatever your role – thank you. (Not forgetting Molly and Mary.)

INTRODUCTION

When I first began to research the history of the US Air Base at Rackheath, I had no idea as to the huge scale of operation that went on there, nor did I realise the major importance it played in the Second World War. It was the closest base we had to Germany.

I was fortunate as I was able to contact the local historian to the 467th, Mr Perry Watts. With the help of his records and his extensive knowledge, the memories and letters of some of the personnel stationed at Rackheath, plus some of the local people who were delighted to take some time to recall memories of their younger days when the 'Boys' were in town, I was able to put this book together.

There are many fascinating stories involving the 467th, some very funny and some very sad. I have chosen the ones I feel will give the reader an insight into the lives of the American airmen and the residents of Rackheath during this torrid and dramatic period of the Second World War, and I hope that the reader will want to go on to seek out the full story behind the 467th Heavy Bombardment Group, American Eighth Air Force.

CONTENTS

FOREWORD

Many tales have been told and stories written about the time in England when we 'Yanks' came to those shores in forces, divisions and groups. We tore down lanes and through the quiet villages in our trucks and jeeps and roared down the concrete strips, so freshly laid over the used-to-be cow pastures, in our thundering Liberators.

Here is an account of one such group, my group, the 467th Bomb Group-Heavy. We were based in a remote eastern corner of England known as Norfolk in the small village of Rackheath. As you will learn, many were the triumphs and defeats, the joys and the sorrows we shared there. In the reading of it, the story and details are quite accurate. I have very vivid memories of so many of the events depicted here. I truly recommend this book as a gate to the inner problems and feelings of the group, the staff and supervision.

As I have mentioned, many pages have been written about our time at Rackheath but this story is unique. It is written by one who grew up in post-war England and whose background is firmly planted in the Norfolk area. It is, I believe, very appropriate that a story of the 467th be told by one so closely associated with the land and its people. Who better to know and understand how we were perceived! David H. Kibble-White is our narrator. He has done an excellent job in the telling.

I shall never forget that spot in that little corner of Norfolk where so much of my life was lived in such a short space of time. Indeed, so strong were the ties that were made, so profound was our mission, we left feeling akin with each other, the land and its people; such bonds can never be broken!

ALBERT J. SHOWER
Colonel, USAF/Ret.

FLAK

Like flowers suddenly bursting into bloom.
Not with the sweet smell of spring. But with
red and yellow centres of death, surrounded
with black petals. Their pollen being deadly
shards of red hot metal thrusting outwards in
search of men and machines. To kill and to
maim, spinning bits of metal that pierce the
thin walls of their sanctuary, getting into the
workings of the engines chewing up its
insides until it becomes useless and dead.
Tearing into the bodies of the men who flew
these warbirds. Tearing and ripping the flesh
and bones away, allowing life's blood to lie
thick on the floor. Destroying young lives,
destroying their hopes and their dreams.
Wrenching them from their loved ones, to
leave them scattered on some foreign soil.

DAVID H. KIBBLE-WHITE

Rackheath Air Base, 1945

CHAPTER ONE

The Making of an Air Base

As a casual traveller taking the A1151 road from Norwich to Wroxham, you will enter after some three miles the small village of Rackheath. On cresting the hill you will see a right hand turn with a signpost bearing the words 'Industrial Estate'. Take a few minutes out of your journey and go down Green Lane, for some six hundred yards, where you will find the entrance to the Estate. Take a look around at the modern-day industry and marvel at the fact that here you could purchase almost anything – a new pram, motor car, boat, get you house double glazed or even buy your custom made furniture. Whilst driving round this estate you cannot help but notice that tucked in amongst the modern factory units there are some old buildings with a distinct military look about them. You will probably wonder why.

Let me take your mind back, back to the dark days of the Second World War, to the Autumn of 1942. You are standing in open fields in the village of Rackheath with a population of less than four hundred souls, the sort of place where everyone knows everyone else, and everyone knows everyone else's business. The village boasted two public houses, two shops, a school and a church, but very little else, agriculture being the mainstay of the day. In truth there are two villages known as Rackheath; there is Rackheath Parva and Rackheath Magna. They are about a mile and a half apart, separated by agricultural land and adjoined only by two narrow lanes, Green Lane and Muck Lane. There was a row of cottages known as Barrack Row between the two villages. Each of the villages kept to itself and each thought it was the better village; there was a great deal of rivalry and jealousy. There was of course a pub in each village. People from the surrounding area treated both Rackheaths as one village and it was only the residents who thought of them as two distinct villages.

In the Autumn of 1942 the local residents were very surprised to see an auto-gyro flying low over the villages. It criss-crossed the houses and farmland for several days on end. Rumours began to abound. What was happening? Was this some new weapon that the Germans had invented to bring terror into their lives? Were they to be invaded? They did not have long to wait. In war time things happen fast. The villagers were told that they were to have an airfield built right on their doorstep; in fact it was to be built on the land between the two villages. This news was received with mixed feelings. The publicans and the shopkeepers could see the benefits; however the residents were outraged as they could see only the dangers it would bring, not only to themselves but to their way of life. With all the strangers that would be wandering around they would feel unsafe. The residents of Barrack Row were even less pleased when they were told that they would have to move as their houses were exactly where the airfield was going to be.

Barrack Row consisted of five cottages, one of which was occupied by Mrs Aggie Curtis and her husband, who together ran one of the local shops. At this point it should be said that the aircraft which eventually came here took the name of 'The Rackheath Aggies', and it has been suggested by some historians that Aggie Curtis was the inspiration for this as she had the reputation of being a lively character in the village. It is however more likely that the name came from a Texas football team.

Prefabs were built in various parts of the village to accommodate the inhabitants of Barrack Row and the cottages were demolished. Mr Engleton, who farmed Dakenham Hall, was also told to move as his herd of Friesian cows grazed in what was to become part of the airfield. The farm buildings were not in the way so they were left intact and are still in use today.

As Barrack Row was demolished, teams of men were brought in to cut down trees which had been marked by the engineers whose job it was to turn these green fields into a great mass of concrete and buildings. Not all these men were outsiders. One or two local men were employed, like Frank Sewel who was later to become foreman of one of the gangs. Ted Webb was another local man employed for this purpose, but in the main, it was outsiders who brought disruption and carnage to this peaceful part of Norfolk.

Having cleared the trees and houses which stood in the way, the next task was to rip up the hedgerows and clear tree stumps to allow the building of three huge runways in a rough, triangular pattern. The main runway was to be built north to south and 6,000 ft in length, with the remaining two runways on a north-east to south-west and south-east to north-west direction. These were to be 4,500 ft in length and 150 ft wide. Massive amounts of heavy machinery were brought in to achieve this mammoth task. Bulldozers and earth movers were used to cut away the soil and to fill in any dips in the landscape. It is said that one of the smaller runways was to run through marshland, and it appears that this caused major difficulties in construction, as no matter how much they filled it, it continued to sink. All sorts of debris was thrown in to try to stop it sinking – broken shovels, broken wheelbarrows and bags of cement that had gone off. When this land was eventually returned to the landowners, this part of the runway was apparently some eleven feet thick.

After the earth movers came huge rollers to compress the chalk base ground. Tons and tons of the rubble used came from the houses and factories that had been bombed in the London blitz. Train load after train load and lorry load after lorry load were brought from out of the area. This rubble was crushed and rolled in readiness for the concrete to make up the runways, perimeter track and hard stands.

Meanwhile on the other side of Green Lane a mammoth building project was going on to construct the living quarters and offices that would house the personnel required to operate this airfield – both ground crew and air crew. Some 2,500 personnel were to live and work here at any one time. By the end of hostilities some 5,000 men and women would pass through this small corner of Norfolk, and that being only in the confines of the airfield itself.

The living quarters for the enlisted men and junior officers would be 'Nissen hut' types of construction. These could be likened to a half barrel made of corrugated steel, turned on its side and fixed over a concrete pad. The ends of the 'barrel' would be filled in with wood, but would incorporate two windows and a door at each end. A wooden porch affair was fitted over the door to try to keep at least some of the draught at bay. The huts would accommodate between twelve and sixteen men in very crowded and, I am sure, very uncomfortable conditions. The heating was by way of a pot bellied stove in the middle of the hut for which a ration of two 56 lb bags of coal per week were allowed. Many of the troops that were to occupy these Nissen huts complained of the lack of heat that the stoves gave out. Unless you stood within a few feet of the stove, you felt no heat at all. The two bags of coal were never enough, so foraging parties were sent out into the woods to gather more fuel, although this was strictly against the rules. Severe penalties would ensue if they were caught. One crew member told me that they would make a mental note during the day where such bounty was to be found and they would slip out after dark to retrieve it. Wooden packing cases were eagerly sought, as was anything else likely to burn; nothing that was considered to be combustible stayed around for very long. In the winter these huts became severe health hazards, as apart from being very cold, the metal shell would freeze, only to drip water when the heat of the stove hit the roof. They would also become steam baths when the men hung up their wet clothes to dry. In the summer of course they became unbearably hot to the point where the men complained they could not breathe.

The senior officers were housed in prefabricated buildings known as 'seco huts' (sectional huts). Only one or two officers were billeted per hut. This type of hut was also used for mess halls, briefing rooms, sick bays and so on. The 'seco' hut could be made to any size or shape when being put together, depending on the needs. This area not only housed the living quarters and general offices that one would expect, but it was also the site for a full hospital, dentist, cinema, gymnasium, clubs, and a private chapel, as well as briefing rooms, showers and general bathroom facilities. Weaving in and out of these buildings bomb blast shelters were dug, these being constructed by digging a deep trench and lining the sides with brickwork with the top left open. The whole site was constructed in the grounds of Sir Edward Stracey's estate which had undulating ground with many trees and shrubs and was away from prying eyes and possible enemy intruders. Site 12 was the first to be completed. This housed many of the Irish labourers who were brought in to help build the airfield. Sanitation on the site was far superior to that of the village, with flush toilets and running water. Reports say that the toilets were the 'honey pot' variety, but this is probably untrue as the sewer system can still be seen today. This part of the site was constructed by Costains, Llewellin and several other contractors.

In the meantime, back across the road, on the main part of the airfield things were going well. Muck Lane had been closed off and ripped up as it ran through the middle of the airfield. The hard-core had been put down and rolled for the runways, and a perimeter track had been laid all the way round the airfield, stretching some 2.2 miles and linking up each end of the runways. Hard stands had been put in place at various intervals around the perimeter track for the aircraft to stand at 'dispersal' points. These were known as spectacle stands, simply because they were shaped like a pair of spectacles to take two planes. It was time to start pouring the concrete for the runways. A huge concrete mixer was built on stilts and a water pump built next to it. The pump could be heard night and day chugging away, drawing enough water to sustain the hungry mouth of the mixer. The concrete was laid in sections using steel shuttering held together with big steel pins. After each section was laid a mastic joint was inserted before the next section was laid. This was used as an expansion joint to stop the concrete rubbing together and breaking up if there was any movement due to a big aircraft bouncing along it, or severe adverse weather that might cause movement. The men building these runways worked very long hours and it

Sir Edward Stracey's Hall, 1945, now a block of flats

The Estate

was back-breaking work. It's not surprising that many of them took several pints at one of the local hostelries after a day's work. There is no evidence of drunkenness recorded in the area, so it seems they could all hold their drink. Miles and miles of drainage and underground electricity cables were laid all round the area. Each runway was to have a lighting system for landing purposes and Rackheath was to have its own independent electricity supply and back-up generators.

The main airfield did not consist only of runways and perimeter track. Two big underground fuel dumps were put in place, each one containing 100,000 gallons of high octane gasoline. One was at the south end of the field, the other was put next to Rackheath railway station. One must wonder at the mind of a man who could put a 100,000 gallon petrol tank next to a railway station in war time and think it safe.

There was a control tower built at the intersection of the runways. Repair shops, stores and a whole host of other buildings were constructed, including two vast hangars measuring some 240 ft long, 150 ft wide and 39 ft high, which would accommodate a plane with its 130 ft wingspan for repair in a hurry. A bomb dump was constructed at the far end of the airfield. This was a simple affair – just a series of trenches bricked up either side and covered by camouflage netting.

By mid 1943, the major part of the building was completed by the main contractor for the entire site, John Laing. It was said that the cost exceeded £1,000,000.

In a few short months the peaceful life of a small country village had been turned upside down. One could see that the natives would be restless when the government of the day decided that they were going to plonk an airfield right in their midst, with the constant noise of the concrete mixer and heavy lorries charging up and down the narrow lane at all times of the day and night and hundreds of strange men taking over the local pubs. It could be seen however that the young ladies of the village would not be too unhappy. Not that it is suggested that anything untoward went on; it was just nice for them to see some fresh faces around the village.

In due course the airfield was turned over to the RAF with a view to becoming operational, but still the local residents had not been told what the base was to be used for. Rumours increased: some thought it was to be a fighter base, others a base for Lancaster bombers. Imagine their surprise then when the Americans arrived. It was only one officer and three enlisted men, but nevertheless they were American – the advance party of 1229th Quartermasters Company. And it began to dawn on the locals that they were to be invaded, not by the Germans as first thought, but by the Americans. Some of the older generation of Rackheath were even more incensed by this. The supposed morals of the Americans were deemed to be very low and many thought, quite wrongly, that no woman would be safe abroad on her own. However several of the younger ladies were quite looking forward to their arrival.

These few Americans started to receive stores and 'kit out' the base, and over the next few months hundreds of American personnel began to arrive at Rackheath. There were dentists, clerks, maintenance men, fire crews and ordnance men complete with a supply of heavy bombs and ammunition. The hospital was to have a surgeon, four medical officers, technicians for the pharmacy, its own laboratory and x-ray unit and ambulance drivers, but there were never any nurses assigned to them. One must wonder who emptied the bedpans?

And so the list went on. By the time the base was fully operational they had everything they wanted, including a bank, shop-cum-café (p.x) and a projectionist for the cinema (there is no mention of an usherette or ice cream girl!).

When the Americans began to take up station it was found that the base was not all that they required, so they set to and built more offices, roads and parking bays. The maintenance men did not have enough room to repair their own vehicles so they built their own service block some 60 ft long.

After all the building had been done, in the first instance by the official MOD then added to by the Americans, there was almost a complete airfield with three long runways, perimeter track, fifty hard stands for the planes to sit at 'dispersal', control tower and all the necessary offices and living quarters the personnel needed to run such a big operation. The only thing they were short of was the aeroplanes, the men to fly them and the men to keep them in the air. No one was sure at this stage when they would arrive.

It was not until December 1943, that a Lt Col Herzberg and an advance party of American officers arrived. Their job was to ensure that the base was fully equipped and settled, to enable the base to become active. (In England it is 'Airfield' or 'Aerodrome', in America 'Air Base'. So from now on Rackheath will be referred to as a base.) When Lt Col Herzberg was satisfied, the base was assigned to the Second Bombardment Division of the Eighth Air Force on 11th March 1944. Lt Col A. Shower was named as station commander, with Lt Col Herzberg as air executive officer with responsibility for operations and intelligence. Lt Col I. S. Walker was appointed ground executive officer.

Prior to all this happening, the first of the assigned aircraft had left Morrison Field in Florida bound for Rackheath. They flew what was known as

The base in winter

the 'southern ferry route'. This would take them via Waller Field, Trinidad, Bellum Brazil, Fortaleza and Natal Brazil, Dakar, Marrakech, Prestwick Scotland, Valley on the isle of Anglesey, North Wales and then onto Rackheath (why they flew from Scotland to North Wales and not direct to Rackheath is unknown). The aircraft assigned to Rackheath was the B-24 Liberator, a heavy bomber that could carry a medium size bomb load and was armed with a fair array of 50 mm calibre guns; they were well able to take care of themselves in battle.

With perfect timing the first of the Liberators flew over Rackheath railway station just as the first of the ground crew that looked after them were disembarking from the train at Rackheath. Again, with perfect timing, this was on the day (11th March) that Lt Col Shower took command. It took several days for all the aircraft to arrive. Sixty had set out from America, but one aircraft and crew were lost in a take-off accident at Agadir, Morocco. A second aircraft crashed into the Atlas Mountains, North Africa. The crew was lost as well.

So of the sixty that set out, fifty-eight landed at Rackheath. Fifty-seven landed safely, but one poor soul tried to land down-wind on one of the shorter runways and wrecked a brand new Liberator. The crew were unhurt, apart from damaged pride. On arriving at Rackheath six aircraft were transferred straight away to other units based in East Anglia. This left fifty-two (including one wrecked plane) to be based at Rackheath. These were then split into four squadrons, the 788th, 789th, 790th and the 791st.

With the arrival of the aircraft and crews, along with ground staff, the base was complete. RAF Rackheath, Station 145, under the control of the 467th Heavy Bombardment Group of the American Eighth Air Force was as author Martin Bowman put it, one of the 'Fields of Little America'.

CHAPTER TWO

'Black Al'

Although all were safely gathered in as far as personnel, aircraft and stores were concerned, the base was by no means ready for action. There were numerous tasks to be carried out before Lt Col Shower could let his men near the enemy. The first disappointment for the men was that they were to be confined to base for the first four weeks. But men being men, it is known that even on the first night a considerable quantity of English beer and rough cider found its way on to the base. It can be imagined what two or three pints of English beer, and especially rough cider, did to those boys; they were not used to strong English ale. And it must be remembered that these were not battle weary veterans, these were young boys, barely out of high school, somewhere between the age of nineteen to twenty-two. The only combat experience they had was to drop a few practice bombs in the desert back home. With the exception of one or two senior officers, not one of them knew what it would be like to fly through a storm of enemy flak, or to be chased and shot at by the mighty Luftwaffe fighters. Of course they had been told what it would be like and they had seen newsreel footage back home. They had trained to take avoiding action as if an enemy plane was on their tail. But they had not faced the real thing. And every man-jack of them was SCARED.

It was during this settling period that the men of the 467th had their first air raid warning. Again they had been told what to do if such a thing happened, but not many of them had taken much notice as they did not think an air raid would take place out in the sticks. Besides, air raids did not take place back home, so why should they here? The result was major confusion with people running in all directions, not knowing where to go or what to do. One crew member recalls the early days at Rackheath.

'We thought the Luftwaffe had about given up bombing Britain when we arrived. But our first days had air raid alerts and this was to take us by complete surprise. For some it was a case of "which way do we run". We heard the uneven droning of German planes for the first time and went out to look. The searchlights all about us stabbed the sky and we could hear the anti-aircraft fire. On the first two raids shell fragments fell on the base. On many of these nights we heard the RAF going out. The roaring of their engines filled the sky and went on for what seemed an eternity.'

But Lt Col Shower was to change all that, and many other things, in double quick time. He was to make sure every man knew his place and knew his job.

Lt Col Shower was to have a major influence on the 467th, the Eighth Air Force in general, and on the village of Rackheath in the months and years to come. He was known as 'Black Al', not because of the colour of his skin, but because he was a very harsh task master.

Albert Joseph Shower was born in Madison, Wisconsin on 16th June 1910. At the age of twenty he became an undergraduate at the University of Nebraska. From there he went to a United States Military Academy, as a cadet officer. He graduated with a Bachelor of Science degree and in 1935 he was commissioned 2nd Lieutenant in the Corps of Engineers. He had pilot training a year later, and was transferred to the Air Corps. He was promoted to 1st Lieutenant on 12th June 1938. After his first assignment in Hawaii he was transferred to Chanute Field, Illinois, and remained there until 1942. He rose to the rank of Captain in September 1940 and to the rank of Major in July 1941. He achieved the rank of Lieutenant Colonel on 23rd January 1942, when only thirty-one years old, one of the youngest colonels in the Air Corps.

During 1942–3, he was stationed in the Southwest Pacific area on the staff of General Harman. He became provisional Group Commander in 1943 in the Second Air Force with a group he took to Africa.

On the 17th September 1943 Lt Col Albert J. Shower joined the 467th Bombardment Group at the AFA school of Applied Tactics at Orlando, Florida, and hence to Rackheath, where he later became a full Colonel.

He was a strict disciplinarian. He believed in shiny shoes, smart dress and, above all, the need for obeying orders. Every Sunday morning those who were not flying had to parade in their dress uniforms on one of the runways for inspection. He insisted that his men trained, and kept on training, all the time he was at Rackheath. When a mission was recalled, or when no missions were ordered for that day, he would send the men up on practise flights to 'camera bomb' parts of Great Britain and to practise evasion tactics from imaginary enemy fighters. On one occasion in August 1944 a crew was practicing over the North Sea when a Sgt Cunningham, upper turret gunner, had a malfunction in his turret and managed to shoot down the lead plane. Col Shower instantly demoted him and he was permanently grounded. Col Shower's aim was to prepare his men for what was to become, for the 467th, a very bloody war from which a great many of them would not return. He wanted to give them the best chance of survival that they could hope for. In his eyes the only way to do this was to learn discipline, obey orders, and train. He was to be proved right.

Many of the men who served under him at Rackheath don't remember meeting him. If they had, they certainly would not have forgotten. But those who did said he was hard but fair. Tch/Sgt Paul Kuchinski (Flight Engineer) remembers the only time he met 'Black Al'. It was at a time when Paul was due to go off on a mission but found, in his opinion, the plane to be unsafe. Whilst arguing with the ground chief who insisted the plane was fit, Paul felt a tap on his shoulder and on turning round there stood Col Shower asking what the problem was. Paul explained to the Colonel that he thought the plane to be unfit and the ground chief thought it to be air worthy. Col Shower instantly ordered the ground chief to bring another plane and never argue with the flight engineer again. He then proceeded to give the ground chief the biggest dressing down Paul had ever heard, telling him that he did not have to put his life on the line whereas the air crew did.

On one occasion, on returning from a mission, some of the aircraft landed at Horsham St Faith because of the fog over Rackheath, and they thought they could not get down safely. The next day the crews had to go back to St Faith to fly their aircraft home. The day was sunny but with persistent patches of fog still around. Because of poor visibility, all the aircraft had to make two or three passes over the base before they could land, but finally they all got down safely and parked on the hard stands when along came Col Shower with Major Taylor CO of the 788th. Col Shower was furious and wanted to see the problem for himself. Calling for a Navigator, Radio Operator and Flight Engineer, he promptly boarded one of the planes and took off. After flying round the area he made an approach to land, with flaps down but wheels up. As the aircraft got lower and lower the crowd, which had now gathered on the airfield to watch, began to wonder if Col Shower knew that he had not lowered his undercarriage, especially as he was only a few feet from the runway. Then at the last minute, just when everybody expected the worst, he boosted the power and pulled up to go around again. He flew round the field a few more times, then set himself up for the landing pattern. As he turned on the approach, he put the plane through a 90 degree bank, a feat no one ever thought a Liberator was capable of. Again Col Shower came down the runway, flaps down but no undercarriage, this time even lower to the ground, so low in fact, that some of the ground crew, who were watching, swear he was no more than four or five feet off the runway. Then, unbelievably, he cut the power and at the very last moment boosted the power and pulled the aircraft up. After one more run at flying a few feet off the ground he lowered his landing wheels and came in for a perfect landing. Parking the aircraft, and without a word being spoken, he left in his staff car. The crew members who flew that exercise with the Colonel said later that they dare not ask if he knew the wheels were not down. They then applied to the stores for clean trousers. Col Shower never asked his men to do something he could not do himself.

Those who watched from the ground said they had never seen such a spectacular flying display and once again it proved that Col Shower knew what he wanted his men to be able to do. It also showed them what a fine aircraft a Liberator was and what it was capable of doing.

There was however another side to Col Shower, and it relates to the school children of Rackheath. Many of them had to walk from the Sole and Heel pub at the bottom of Green Lane, past the base to the top of the lane to go to school (it's still in use today) a distance of a mile and a half. As there were big lorries going up and down this narrow lane all day, the parents of the children were naturally concerned that someone was going to get injured or even killed. They approached Col Shower and explained the situation. He immediately ordered that two lorries would pick up the children at the Sole and Heel and transport them to and from school. When Norfolk Education heard about this they told the Colonel to stop doing it as it was not in his domain. The Colonel was so incensed by this he promptly requisitioned Green Lane and put a picket guard at each end. Thereafter anyone wanting to use Green Lane had to have a pass from the military, everyone, that is, except the local children.

Eric Fiddy, as a lad, would cycle with his parents from Horsham St Faith to see some friends in Salhouse every Sunday. On reaching Green Lane they would have to get a pass from the guard at the top of the lane, cycle down and hand the pass in to the guard at the bottom of the lane. Eric well remembers the events: 'They seemed to be very big men to me, with these big white funny helmets on. Of course they were the full helmet as worn by American servicemen, unlike the saucer helmet worn by English troops. They stood there with a gun and looked very menacing. Because of their helmets my dad always called them "snowdrops". They were always very friendly towards us, but they still worried me.'

The lorries continued to pick the children up until finally the education committee gave in and provided a bus to transport the children to school. Making provision for school children in this period of uncertainty, when his men were fighting a war, seems the mark of a man who wished so very hard to see the whole thing through without trying to destroy anyone's way of life.

As a final pointer to the iron rod that Col Shower used to rule the men of the 467th, we come back to the plane mentioned in the previous chapter – the one that landed down wind on arriving at Rackheath. Remember, these pilots were inexperienced, they were just completing a long haul to a strange country, a strange base. It was a mistake that any pilot could make given the situation. 2nd Lt Elroyd Beaney was tired and nervous. He had brought his crew thousands of miles and was more than relieved to see the base stretch out below him. He had done numerous hours flying in the desert practising bomb runs. The base on which he trained had been in the desert with no hills and no contours in the ground. But now he was surrounded by trees, undulating ground and a strange base. He wanted the landing to be perfect. His big mistake was not looking at the sock to check wind direction. He lined the aircraft up to make the perfect landing, not too much speed with just the right amount of flaps to touch down nice and smooth. It was only then he realised that he was running out of runway, down wind and with no hope of stopping in time. He did the only thing he could do, he stood on the brakes and because he was braking so hard, he snapped off the front wheel, thus allowing the aircraft to drop on to its nose, totally wrecking a brand new Liberator. He was hauled up before Col Shower, who, after many choice expletives, put him on punishment and promptly demoted him to second pilot. When Col Shower was asked about the incident many years later he said 'Bloody young fool, but I could not be too hard on him, he was such a damned good pilot.' Elroyd was to spend the next few weeks as a co-pilot, but was then re-tested and given back his command.

During this 'settling in' period Col Shower ordered more practise flights over the English countryside, to enable his men to become accustomed to terrain similar to that which they would find in Europe. At the same time, there were maps and charts to be studied. Some of the men were sent to other established USAF bases in East Anglia to see how it was all done. Life was very hectic for all the personnel. On the lighter side, the men were having a great deal of difficulty getting used to the blackout and kept tripping over things when going from one hut to another in the dark. Many of them said they could not get over how green everything was after spending so long in the desert. Meanwhile mail began to arrive and many began to figure out a way to beat the censorship and let their loved ones know where they were. Movies were shown, although it was said that the Nissen Hut was not the ideal cinema as the acoustics left a lot to be desired, giving little illusion to Hollywood romance.

[24]

Finally, on 10th April 1944, training became reality. This was the day of the first mission for the 467th. The target was to be an aircraft assembly plant at an airfield in Bourges, France. Thirty aircraft were to be dispatched. Many said their prayers in earnest that day.

Col Shower in *Little Pete*

CHAPTER THREE

In Action

Col Shower himself was to lead the two group squadrons. The Colonel flew in the first squadron and Lt Col Walter Smith led the second squadron. They had an uneventful trip to the target, with all planes reaching their destination (which was not always the case). All but four of the aircraft dropped their cargo of six 1,000 lb s.a.p. (semi armour piercing) bombs on the target. These four had mechanical problems and could not unload their bombs. Results later judged the bombing pattern to be 'very good', with only one aircraft's bombs falling outside the target area. The return journey was just as uneventful; no flak was encountered and they did not see any German fighters. The group returned to Rackheath amid blue skies and bright sunshine. A great number of the personnel gathered around the perimeter track to greet the returning crews and aircraft. The ground crews anxiously peered into the sky to see if any of their charges were damaged. But everything was fine, no bits hanging off, no holes to patch up and no engines smoking or showing signs of damage. Col Shower led the group over the base in perfect formation before coming in to land. Thirty aircraft were sent out, thirty aircraft came home, much to the delight and relief of those who had stayed behind. The 467th had completed their first mission in style. They had flown their first 'milk run'.

On the following day they were to fly their second mission and their first into Germany, with thirty-six aircraft made up into three squadrons. This was to prove a very different story.

All thirty-six aircraft were dispatched on time. They were to be part of a nine-hundred-strong bomber force assembling over the North Sea. The remainder of the force were B-17s and B-24s from other bases in the area. Their aim was to destroy the Focke-Wolf aircraft factories in Ascherleben, East Germany. Lt Col Herzberg was to lead the group.

The outward journey was uneventful until they reached their 'run in' point over the target. Suddenly a great barrage of flak appeared in front of them, shells bursting so close together that it seemed impossible for

Waiting for the return

After the first mission

anything to fly through such a storm and come out the other side in one piece. But by this time the bombardier had control of the aircraft and he, lying full length in the nose of the aircraft with his eyes glued to the bomb sight, was unable to see the flak. It was his job to guide the aircraft over the target and let the bombs go at just the right moment. The pilot would not have been able to take avoiding action as he could only take orders from the bombardier, and not until the bombardier had said the words 'bombs away' over the intercom could the pilot respond to the situation in front of him and get them out of the range of fire.

Several of the aircraft sustained damage, and two men were wounded. As the aircraft emerged from the flak they spotted enemy fighters, but for some unexplained reason the fighters did not press home an attack. The raiders turned and headed for home. Some of the aircraft were having difficulty keeping up with the main stream due to the extent of their damage.

On returning to England the first Rackheath plane was lost. *Devil's Hostess* had been hit several times, causing severe damage. Lt Jack Skinner had coaxed the aircraft back over the coast at Cromer and he and his crew thought that they would make it. He was just eight miles from safety and on his final approach path when he could hold the plane no longer. He was going down and there was nothing he could do about it. They were too low for the crew to bale out safely; he attempted a 'belly' crash land. Unfortunately he misjudged it and crashed on to a bungalow in Stalham, killing himself and six of his crew. Three did survive: the Radio Operator, Ball Turret Gunner and one Waist Gunner. These were the first of many casualties the 467th were to endure. The bungalow was destroyed, but fortunately it was unoccupied at the time.

Several more missions were flown over the next few days, although a number of these were recalled, usually because of bad visibility over the target area.

On 22nd April 1944 the 467th took off for their tenth mission. They were to strike at the marshalling yards of Hamm. However events were to go wrong from the start. The 467th were again to be part of a large formation. The crews had been awakened at 0200 hrs as normal. Briefings and weather forecasts had been gone through, breakfast had been eaten and equipment drawn. But the weather over the target was not suitable at the time take-off should have begun, so a delay was ordered. When they later got the order to go, it was cancelled almost as soon as it was issued and this happened several times during the day. By the time Bomber Command finally sanctioned the mission it was well into the afternoon. The crews had been dressed in flying gear and had been hanging round their planes for most of the day. Nerves were very frayed at this point and many of them

Marshalling Yards, Hamm

could not have taken another cancelled order. When the order finally came down they were told that the weather was still very marginal over the target. The crews were also aware that because of the delay, they would be returning home in the failing light. Many had a sense of foreboding.

The divisional formations circled over Cromer to gain their instructed flying height and to form up with the rest of the bomber stream. They headed south, crossing the channel towards Holland to rendezvous with the P-38 Lightnings which were to escort them as far as Dortmund.

The outward journey was without serious incident with only the occasional flak barrage and very little fighter opposition. Hamm, however, was very well defended. The head winds were very strong, slowing the bomber stream down, and the zigzag course they were taking in an effort to try to fool the German radar of their intentions meant that quite a few aircraft were way off course. For those still on course it was early evening and clear weather when the bombers identified their target, some three miles long and half a mile wide. They felt they could not miss. When the Germans

realised the bombers' intentions the defences opened up with great feroc-
ity and accuracy, and enemy fighters were scrambled to harass the
bombers when they left the target.

Those which had strayed off course found themselves over the Ruhr
Valley and were subjected to more intense flak, delaying their approach
even further. As a result, part of the formation missed the target alto-
gether. The 445th and the 453rd were prevented from bombing owing to
other incoming groups. Those who could not bomb the primary target
were ordered to fly down the Rhine and bomb an important bridge at
Koblenz. All in all, the whole thing had been a complete shambles and the
crews just wanted to go home. But worse was to come.

On the homeward journey they were all aware that fighters had been
sent to intercept them and every man was ordered to keep his eyes peeled.
Most knew that the mission was a fiasco so nerves were even more ragged
and every movement in the sky seemed like an enemy fighter out to get just
'their' plane and nobody else. As they crossed the coast it was getting dark,
but the tail gunner in *Vadie Raye* (448th), saw German fighters taking off
from bases all along the coast. He reported it to his captain who in turn
passed it on to the group commander and requested fighter support.

The skies over England were fairly clear; there was no moon but the
stars shone brightly. Night flying with hundreds of aircraft in the air at the
same time was hazardous at the best of times, but these were daylight
bombers and their pilots had not been trained in night flying. They were
also not aware that lights on their aircraft were not the right colour code
for night flying. To the ground spotters they were enemy aircraft and were
to be fired on. The coastal ack-ack batteries opened fire. The one big fault
with the Liberator was that it gave off a huge flame from the exhaust thus
enabling it to be spotted and targeted very easily.

Meanwhile the Luftwaffe pilots had mingled in with the homeward
planes. The Liberators kept their lights on, whereas the Germans had
turned theirs off, thus allowing them to be largely unseen and giving them
greater depth to manoeuvre within the flight to press home an attack.
They did this with deadly accuracy and there were many tragic deaths.

Landing procedure was for the returning aircraft to pick up a homing
beacon at low altitude, just south of Cromer, go out to sea at about 1,500
ft, make a 180 degree turn for positive identification to the coastal anti-aircraft batteries, then return inland at the same height and disperse to their
respective bases. However, as they were flying with the wrong colour code
lights, the coastal guns opened fire. At least one Liberator was lost this way.
Lt Cherry Pitts of the 448th took a direct hit and exploded in mid air. It was
later discovered that the British gunners had spotted the intruders that had

followed them back across the channel. They were identified as Me-410s and Ju-88s, but because they were mixed in with the returning B-24s, it was impossible for the ground gunners to take clear and decisive action.

Mr Jack Taylor, a member of the Observer Corps, was on duty that night at Beccles. 'I went on duty that night at 10 o'clock, and was told that some American bombers would soon be returning. I saw them in the distance with their tail lights on, I could hear the drone of their engines as they flew over. Suddenly there was a different engine noise and a Ju-88 flew low overhead, followed by a Me-410. I could see the tracer bullets ripping through the bombers over the Beccles area. One Liberator crashed near the school at Barsham. Another one fell on the railway line at Worlingham. I was the first to report to our centre that enemy aircraft were in the vicinity and they replied that there are no hostile planes on the chart. I heard other sounds of hostile aircraft; again I reported it and again I got the same reply. I was very worried, knowing that all the bombers were coming home and being shot out of the sky. They were sitting ducks. I can only assume the German planes came in under our Radar.'

What Mr Taylor had seen was the Luftwaffe causing mayhem amongst the home-comers. The Liberators were being shot out of the sky at the time they were trying to come into landing patterns, this being their most vulnerable time. The fight was not all one sided. The gunners from the Liberators were shooting at the Germans with some success. But alas, in the confusion, some of the damage done to the Liberators was from other Liberators. It seems the gunners fired at anything that moved, and only afterwards did they ask 'are you friend or foe?'

Some of the early arrivals had not encountered the interlopers at this stage and were preparing to land at Rackheath. The landing lights were switched on and the group prepared for a landing pattern when suddenly the lights were switched off and the crews were told that enemy aircraft were in the area and the landing would have to be delayed. This caused more problems for the pilots as some were very low on fuel while others had taken a battering over the target or from coastal ack-ack guns.

Col Shower recalls that he made three approaches to the runway but the landing lights went out before he could touch down and he had to go round again. At this point he ordered all aircraft to break off into single elements and try to land when they could. One aircraft did manage to get down, but while it was rolling along the runway it was attacked by the enemy and three of the crew were injured. A second plane (*Slugger Joe*) was also attacked as it was trying to land. It took damage to No. 4 engine and had to make an emergency landing with the engine vibrating badly. The third casualty was *Osage Express* from the 790th Squadron. It was half way along the runway when it was attacked by enemy cannon fire, but the upper turret managed to fire some bursts at the enemy before the B-24 slewed off the runway after one of its wheels had dropped into a bomb crater. The front wheel snapped off causing the B-24 to drop on to its nose, resulting in considerable damage to the nose, engines and propellers. Fortunately it finished clear of the runway. *Osage Express* was repaired and returned to active service but was shot down after a few more missions.

Enemy aircraft from other *Luftwaffe Gruppen* were thought to be in the area and it was later learned that one of these planes, a Ju-88, had flown up the length of the runway and dropped bombs. One fell on the edge of a dispersal point, while another fell on the perimeter track killing Private Dan Miney as he cycled back to the main building (a plaque dedicated to him adorns the building where he usually worked and is still in place today). A third bomb was dropped near a Liberator that was undergoing repair and it received damage to the tail and fuselage. One of the maintenance men was injured. A bomb was dropped on a bungalow near the Sole and Heel public house but it failed to go off. It destroyed the bungalow, but as luck would have it the occupants, a woman and her child, had gone next door to seek shelter when the alarm sounded.

All in all five bombs were dropped on Rackheath causing a considerable amount of damage. Thankfully this was the only time the base and village were ever attacked during the hostilities.

The aircraft that was shot down near the school at Barsham near Beccles was flown by Lt Stalie Reid. Lt Reid's aircraft had taken more than its fair share of damage over the target, and had then been attacked by fighters. Lt Reid knew they would not make it home. They were on fire and losing altitude at an alarming rate. He told his crew to bale out while he would stay at the controls to hold the aircraft straight and level for as long as he could. Four of the crew managed to bale out, but sadly Lt Reid and five others could not and they perished. Of the four who did manage to get out, Sgt Hoke died when his parachute opened. The fire had burnt through his harness and with the force of the 'chute' opening, it snapped the harness completely and Sgt Hoke fell out. His body was recovered the next day at Ringstead, several miles from the crash sight. The others landed safely, although with considerable burns. Waist gunner Mervin Shanks remembers that a lady farmer found them and applied dressings soaked in cold tea to the burns, but he cannot remember who she was or where she lived. An appeal was put out to try to find her but to no avail.

The plane came down just yards away from the school, but as it was evening there were no pupils. The plane nose-dived into the ground with such force that the tail section broke off and bounced back across the road, landing beside two cottages.

Denis Sporle was an eleven year old boy at the time. He remembers the incident very clearly. To use his words: 'It was as though it was yesterday. We used to live in the cottage at the back of the school. To get to it you went down a little lane at the side of the school. It was a Saturday night; we kids had taken a bath in the old tin bath in front of the fire and then mother tucked us up in bed. I must have dropped off to sleep, because the next thing I remember was mother shaking me and telling me to come down stairs as fast as I could. I remember hearing gunfire and lots of noise. I ran down the stairs and mother pushed me under the table along with my two sisters. We then heard a big bang and a rumble that sounded like thunder and a few minutes later father rushed in and said a plane had crashed in the meadow across the road. He was a special constable at the time and had been on duty at Ink Factory Hill, about a mile up the road. He had seen the plane on fire and thought it was going to crash on our house, so he had run all the the way home. The next morning we walked up the lane to

Bomb dump

go to church. I saw what remained of the aircraft in the meadow and saw the tail was down by the side of the houses where the Chilvers and Old Mrs Porter lived. The one thing that got to me the most was the horrible smell. I think it was a mixture of fuel, cordite and burnt flesh, although I did not know that at the time. To me it just smelt sickening; it's a smell I will never forget. I can still smell it today.'

Denis still pays homage to those lads who lost their lives in that crash and he has planted hundreds of daffodils on the site, at his own expense. Those who pay a visit in springtime cannot help but admire the beautiful carpet of flowers laid down as an everlasting memorial to these boys. While planting some bulbs a couple of years ago he dug up a 50 mm cannon shell and said it still had that awful smell that he remembers so vividly. Denis was also the driving force behind a memorial stone situated next to the school, which now serves as the village hall. He and a few friends got together to raise the money and have it sited. When this memorial was blessed, the residents of Barsham were pleased to have amongst their congregation one of the survivors from that crash – Waist gunner Sgt Mervin Shanks. Sadly Mervin was the only one of the three survivors of the crash to go through the war. The other two died about a month later on another mission.

On that fateful night the Eighth Air Force lost seventeen aircraft to enemy planes or flak, although some crashed through lack of fuel. The 467th lost seventeen men and had four wounded. An RAF Mosquito was also shot down. It had just taken off from RAF Swannington and it crashed at Ludham, killing both of the crew.

Enemy losses were one Me-410, shot down by B-24 gunners belonging to the 443rd, and an Me-410 flown by Major Dietrich Puttfarken, commander of *Il Gruppe, Kamfgeschwader (KG) 51 Edelweiss (Hornet)*. It is not known where the Major crashed. He was badly shot up and attempted to return to his base in Holland, but never made it. It is believed he crashed into the sea but neither his plane nor his body were ever recovered. The Me-410 which was shot down by the Liberator crashed at Ashby St Mary, some eight miles south of Norwich. The pilot did not survive.

CHAPTER FOUR

The B-24 Liberator

Many of us, when we think of American wartime bombers, think of the B-17, the Flying Fortress. After all, most films feature the B-17 so it has become a familiar picture in our minds. The B-24 Liberator, however, was a far superior aircraft to the Flying Fortress. It is said that the Liberator could fly higher, faster, carry a bigger bomb load and take more punishment than any other bomber in the American Air Force. It was no wonder then that more Liberators were built than any other aircraft.

The Liberator first came to fame as a result of a raid on the oil fields of Ploesti in Rumania, on the 1st August 1943. This mission required crews to fly long distances at low level and drop their bombs into what, in modern day terms, would be called 'the pickle barrel' – in other words precision bombing. They did this with a great deal of accuracy. Unfortunately this particular mission was a disaster and did not achieve what was first claimed. Far too many aircraft and crews were lost unnecessarily. Fifty-two aircraft failed to return and a third of the crews taking part had either been killed, wounded or taken prisoner. Within three weeks the oil refinery was working again to full capacity. It is a tragic story and several books have been written about this mission.

The B-24 Liberator was made by Consolidated Air Corporation, Douglas Aircraft Company, Ford Motor Aircraft Company and North American Aviation Inc. It had a wingspan of some 110 ft, was 66 ft 4 ins in length and 17 ft 11 ins high. It was driven by four Pratt & Witney R-1830 engines, each producing 1,200 hp, with a top speed of 303 mph at 30,000 ft and could carry a bomb load of 8,000 lbs. Its range was 2,100 miles fully laden. Unlike the B-17, it had twin fins or rudders on its tail section.

The B-24 was very well armed with a total of ten 50 mm calibre machine guns, two in the nose, two in the upper turret, two in the lower turret, one for each waist gunner and two in the tail. It was a formidable battle wagon; several of them flying in tight formation could put up a wall of fire in any direction that would spell disaster for any but the bravest of fighter pilots.

Liberators in action

It carried a crew of ten, although this was later reduced to nine. Unlike British planes the Americans carried a co-pilot as well as a pilot, along with a navigator, bombardier, radio operator, engineer/top turret gunner, a ball or bottom turret gunner, two waist gunners and a tail gunner. It was common practice for most if not all the crew to be able to fly the plane. Should the pilot and co-pilot become ill or be injured in any way, some member of the crew could bring the plane home safely.

The B-24 proved to be so versatile that it was used in many theatres of war. Because it could fly successfully at low level it was to adopt a role as a submarine spotter. This was especially true of those used by the RAF. By the end of the war a great many of these aircraft were to carry the roundels of the British and Commonwealth Air Forces.

It was also used as a transport tanker ferrying petrol and supplies. This happened with the 467th. It was used for reconnaissance and for the dropping of agents and supplies behind enemy lines. I think however the most unusual role for the Liberator was as an assembly ship.

Not all aircraft that were damaged could be repaired at Rackheath. Because of the pressure of putting up a full complement of aircraft on a mission, an aircraft that was going to be out of commission for more than a few days was shipped off to RAF Watton, either in bits or, if possible, flown there.

Watton was the main service base for the Eighth Air Force. The spares for those that could be repaired on the base would be trucked from Watton, but if an aircraft was sent to Watton, another aircraft would be sent to replace it and the original aircraft, once repaired, could be shipped out to a new home. For this reason, on reading the full history of the Eighth Air Force, the same aircraft can be seen to be in more than one squadron or group during its career. This was true of several aircraft at Rackheath. Their service records showed that they were members of another squadron or group at sometime in their lives.

In early September 1944, the 467th was stood down from their bombing routine to take up a support role for the allied troops already fighting in France after the D-Day landings. At this stage General Patton's ground forces had an array of tanks, jeeps and numerous other motorised vehicles in France and Belgium. They needed petrol and spares in great quantities. This is where the Liberators of the 467th came in.

The bomb bay no longer carried bombs but specially constructed petrol tanks. On 19th September the 467th set up a base on the recently captured air base at Clastres, Northern France. It seems ironic that just one month earlier the 467th had been bombing this same air base, which at the time was in the hands of the Luftwaffe. American personnel, along with French civilians, filled in the bomb craters, repaired the buildings and generally restored the base to serviceable use.

It would take quite a time for an aircraft first to load up with petrol and supplies at Rackheath, then to fly to France and unload and quite often the crew would not be free to return until after dark. As night flying was not allowed at the time, many of the crews had to do a 'stop over' on French soil. This was a golden opportunity for many of them to make a quick dash to Paris, which had only just been liberated. Many returned with wild and possibly exaggerated stories of the Parisian girls and their exploits. For this reason there was often an array of passengers logged on particular aircraft, who were not strictly allowed. Many did see France in this fashion. Sgt Kuchinski tells a story of when his pilot and co-pilot disappeared on one of these sightseeing missions. 'We had to stop over one night in France so we drew lots as to who was going to guard our ship and who was to get to see a bit of the night life. As usual I drew the short straw and had to stay with the ship and the rest of the crew fled off in all directions with strict instructions to be back by 0700 in the morning. Well, come morning, all the crew were back except the skipper and co-jockey. We had been given instruction to take-off. I did not know what to do. I stalled as much as I could but was ordered to get into pattern. I fired up the ship and started to taxi. I told John Logan that when we got to the end of the runway, I would have to find some way to abort. But luck was on my side; as we neared the end of the taxi way I saw the skipper and the co-pilot running across the grass from the corner of the field to try and catch us. I fiddled with the controls a bit to make one engine backfire to slow us down. It was a mad scramble to get them in the door without being seen. I remember the skipper sitting on the floor grinning from ear to ear saying what a wonderful night he'd had. All the way back to Rackheath he was grinning like a Cheshire cat but no amount of coaxing would get him to reveal what he had been up to.'

Sometimes two flights a day took off from Rackheath with their much needed cargo. They were so successful they had managed to ship over 650,000 gallons of fuel in the first two weeks of operation.

These flights were to go on day after day until October 1944 when they were rotated back to their normal duties. This was by no means the end of the petrol transport: another group would have taken over. I suppose this could be described as a 'rest mission'. Rest, that is, from the strain and anguish of facing flak and enemy fighters day after day.

Another role the Liberator undertook was that of 'Assembly Ship'. At Rackheath this aircraft was known as Pete the POM Inspector, or *Big Pete*; other bases had their own pet names. *Big Pete* was a war weary aircraft, not suitable for bombing missions. It was stripped of its 'fighting gear' and was painted with big yellow spots over its entire surface area. The rear gun turret was removed and a bank of lights fitted in its place.

When a mission was scheduled, perhaps twenty or thirty aircraft were to take-off at the same time. Precision timing was required to get them airborne without accidents. The general procedure was for the first aircraft to take-off and turn to the right. The next aircraft would be rolling down the runway by the time the first aircraft was lifting off, somewhere between fifteen and thirty seconds later. The second aircraft would turn to the left, the next to the right and so on. This was because, as the take-offs were so close together, the aircraft just taking off would have been affected by the 'PropWash' of the one in front if they took off in a straight line. The end result was – all the aircraft airborne but scattered. This is where *Big Pete* came into the equation.

Big Pete would take off first, then fly in ever increasing circles. Each aircraft as it took off would latch on to *Big Pete*'s tail. He was relatively easy to spot because of the brightly painted spots and its bank of tail lights. He would continue to fly in circles until such time as he had gathered in his flock, which would take about an hour depending on how many he had to find. He would stay with the formation until they had reached the correct height and position and would then lead them towards the splashier beacon just south of Cromer. Their height and speed were of vital importance if they were joining other wings from nearby bases. The assembly map opposite would have been issued to every navigator.

As radio silence was the order of the day, *Big Pete* had the help of *Little Pete*, this being a P-47 Thunderbolt. *Little Pete* was in effect the 'sheep dog'. He would scoot around the stragglers and, with a combination of hand signals and flares, would gather them up into a tight formation ready for them to set out across the North Sea. Both *Big Pete* and *Little Pete* would then return to base.

There is an incident recorded about the day *Little Pete* got a bit too enthusiastic in trying to shepherd his charges into formation. It happened on a practise flight, and *Little Pete* was flown that day by Major Walter Smith. As mentioned, *Little Pete*'s job was to scoot around and shuffle the stragglers into position using hand signals. On this particular day *Little Pete* got a bit too close and collided with *Lonely Heart* flown by Lt E. Rice, resulting in *Lonely Heart* having its nose taken off with the unfortunate death of nose gunner Sgt Dadig. *Little Pete* was badly damaged forcing Major Smith to bale out. *Little Pete* crashed and was totally destroyed; Major Smith parachuted to the ground safely. *Lonely Heart* managed to land safely minus her nose thanks to the skill of her pilot, Lt Rice. There were no other injuries.

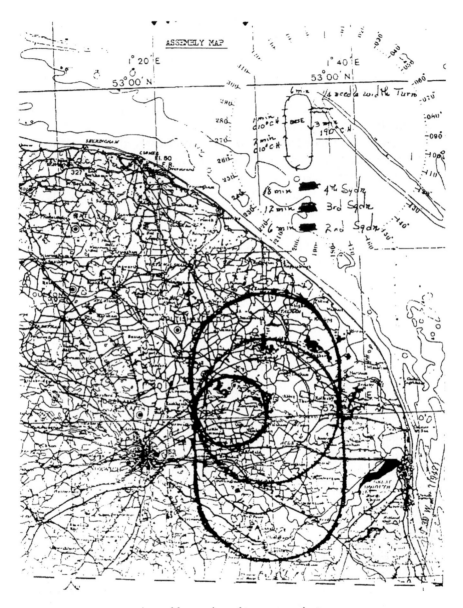

Assembly map issued to every navigator

Lonely Heart's ground crew patched up the damage left by the missing nose section, with bits of wood and canvas and she was later flown to RAF Watton for major surgery. She successfully had a new nose grafted on and returned to active service at Rackheath where she was to fly many more successful missions. *Lonely Heart* survived the war and returned to the United States at the end of hostilities. As for Major Smith, he was banned from flying the new *Little Pete* when it arrived.

It has also been recorded that *Big Pete* went on a mission. It was on Christmas Eve and the mission was to Daun-Gerolstein. Every plane that could fly was put into the air. *Big Pete* was flown by volunteers, the pilot was Lt Charley McMahon. Charley had already completed his 'tour' of missions and would have been able to return home. Such men were known as 'Happy Warriors'. However, he chose to fly *Big Pete*, his only armaments were carbine rifles fired from the waist windows. Fortunately both Charley and *Big Pete* returned safely.

Lt Murphy's B-24H damaged on 8 May, 1944

CHAPTER FIVE

Strange but True

Many stories could be told of the missions of the 467th, and to list them all would require a book thicker than *War and Peace*. However, certain 'odd' stories need to be told.

One of the strangest is of the aircraft known as *Tangerine*, flown by Lt Bill Dillon. On the way back from a mission to Berlin, they were over the North Sea. Fuel was very low and they were sure they would not make it home in their present state. So Bill called for a vote from his crew, 'should they ditch in the sea or try to make it back?' All the crew knew that a Liberator was not the best of aircraft in the sea as it tended to break up very quickly. So the vote was to get home. This meant throwing everything out of the aircraft that would move to try to lighten the load. So everything started going out, parachutes, ammunition, guns and anything else they could lay their hands on. The waist gunners were to throw out their guns and spare ammunition. Everyone was busy with their task when someone noticed that a waist gunner was missing. Sgt James should have thrown out his gun but for some reason he had gone too. They were only five miles from the English coast at the time. Whether he lost his nerve and jumped, knowing that if they ditched in the sea, the chances of him getting out were remote or whether he fell when he threw his gun out, no one knows. He should have had a safety strap attached to his belt to prevent this. The crew said 'he was there one minute, the next minute he had gone'. Lt Dillon contacted Coastal Air Sea Rescue, but no trace of him was ever found.

Tangerine did make it back to landfall, but had to land at Ludham, some twelve miles from home. So short were they on fuel, that, as the plane touched down on the runway, all four engines stopped. The aircraft had to be towed off the runway. That's what's known as cutting it fine.

Even today Lt Dillon has no idea what happened on that flight. *Tangerine* went on to fly many more missions before she crashed and burned out on the 9th September 1944. The pilot was Lt Virgil J. Reinders. They were flying a 'petrol mission' at the time. Lt Reinders was not listed as a pilot on the staff of the 467th and there is no information as to where he came from or what happened to him.

As a footnote, Lt Dillon went on to fly the 'Black Liberators' in the 801st. These Liberators were unarmed machines which were responsible for dropping supplies, agents and arms behind enemy lines. They were stripped of all their fire power, given extra boost power for more speed and would normally carry a skeleton crew of five. The entire 788th squadron was transferred to these missions and a new squadron was to take up residence at Rackheath in the guise of the 788th.

Staff Sgt Paul Hatten tells of another strange incident. 'We were not aware that superstition could possibly affect a mission' he said, 'but thanks to my lovely wife it did just that. When I left home to come overseas, my wife gave me a cameo ring. I wore this ring at all times and I refused to remove it for any reason. We were preparing *Slick Chick* at dispersal for a mission. We all had our flying suits on, and as I was putting on my flak jacket, I noticed the setting had fallen out of the ring. I casually mentioned it to the crew. Suddenly without conversation we were all crawling on our hands and knees in the grass, searching for this stone, but without success.

'As if just to prove a point, I guess we encountered the worst flak we had ever seen. It was very intense and very accurate. Quite a bit of it found our plane. We dropped our bombs on an oil storage tank at Lille in France. We limped back to England with quite a number of holes and a few bits missing from our aircraft. When Lt White got out of the plane, he came over to me and put his arm round my neck and said, "please don't wear any more rings". My answer was "yes sir". That was our fourteenth mission on August 3rd 1944.'

The next unusual mission for *Slick Chick* was on 6th August. Sgt Hatten takes up the story again. 'We took off on a mission for Hamburg, Germany. Lt Doole, our co-pilot, got sick when we were taking off. Lt White told him to go to the nose of the plane and use the nose wheel hatch if he was going to vomit. The smell of vomit inside the plane would have been unbearable all the way to the target and back again. But for some unexplained reason Lt Doole came up the bomb bay and opened the bomb doors to vomit. He stepped on to the catwalk, which was only four inches wide; he must have passed out, because the next thing we knew, he had fallen out. The bombardier tried to catch him, but missed him. We were three thousand feet over the English Channel at the time. He must have regained consciousness on the way down, because we saw his 'chute' partially open during his descent, but it did not break his fall. We flew at sea level for three hours with Air Sea Rescue, but we could not find him.'

Sunday 16th August, was another of *Slick Chick*'s frightening episodes.

[43]

Slick Chick

Gunner's Crew
(l to r) ?; William Ulman, John Logan,
Rufus Webb, Marvin Fritsch, Paul Kuchinski

Paul Kuchinski (left), John Logan, Christmas,
1944

Sgt Hatten takes up the story. 'The purpose of this mission, was to drop 1,000 lb demolition bombs on the German lines in France. According to briefing, we were not supposed to encounter flak, but the Germans had moved in very heavy Ack Ack guns on railway flat cars. Five minutes before the target the lead plane, flown by Lt Leyes, took a direct hit in the bomb bay, breaking the plane in half. I saw one "chute" and there were unconfirmed reports of others.

'A piece of Lt Leyes plane caught in the leading edge of our wing. Lt White gave the warning to jump and we all hooked up our parachutes as fast as we could, because only the pilot and co-pilot have back pack "chutes". They use them to sit on. We all had chest "chutes" which we carried loose with us. If a tail or ball gunner tried to wear his "chute", he would never fit in the turrets. By some miraculous feat Lt White gained control of the plane after we had dropped out of formation, and we dropped our bombs in the channel and tried to return to base.'

Slick Chick was badly damaged, with a large hole in the left wing and a large piece of Lt Leyes bomber stuck in the leading edge. This caused the plane to be out of trim and wing heavy. Flying such a monster was almost impossible but Lt White did manage to coax *Slick Chick* home to Rackheath without injury to any of his crew.

Sgt Hatten goes on to say: 'The enlisted men of Lt Leyes crew lived with our crew in the same hut. It was very lonesome and quiet that night and we did not feel much like talking. There were no confirmed survivors and we were sure nobody could live through that. But about forty years later, I read an unbelievable report. When Lt Leyes plane was shot down and we watched it break up, Lt Leyes and his co-pilot Lt Coolridge were blown free of the aircraft still sitting in their seats with seat belts still attached. The explosion had knocked them unconscious. When they regained their senses, they managed to release their seats and parachuted to the ground. They were caught and made POWs for the duration of the war.'

Ball gunner/armourer Sgt Walter Munday, remembers the day they were returning from a mission. The aircraft had been damaged by the intense flak they had encountered over the target. It had left a gaping hole just behind the rear gunner's turret. Boxes of ammunition that were stored there began to explode in all directions and they were in danger of being shot down by their own plane. Red hot tracers were going everywhere, 50 mm cannon shells were bursting and the rear gunner could not leave his turret for fear of being shot by his own ammunition. A hasty decision was made to land at RAF Woodbridge, this being the nearest emergency base capable of taking a B-24. The rear turret gunner was eventually released unharmed and I think this is the only time a rear gunner felt the safest place in a Liberator was his own turret. The crew must have been touched by the hand of God that day because no member of the crew was injured.

Several of the crews did have lucky mascots which they carried with them on missions. They were anything from a lock of hair from a girlfriend or wife, to a silk handkerchief or a simple elastic band, in fact anything that gave them comfort or security.

One of Walter Mundy's crew always took an old greasy cap with him on his missions. This crew member was the nose gunner and it was his standard practice to leave the nose on landing and make his way to the centre of the aircraft. On this particular day he left his cap in the nose of the aircraft, and the cap fell out when the front was lowered. The poor chap was distraught and was afraid to fly without it. So much so that he would have faced court martial rather than go without his cap, but it was his lucky day, for someone found it and handed it in to the guardroom later that day.

Lt Frank Summers tells of his first combat mission. It was usual for new pilots to Rackheath to fly their first mission as co-pilot to a more experienced crew and Lt Summers was no exception. 'It was November 12th 1944 I was co-pilot for David Nash and we were going to Aschen on a bombing mission to support advancing troops. The flak was pretty bad; we lost two engines almost as soon as it started and later on we lost a third, but we did manage to get our bombs on the target. It was clear we were not going to get home, so we headed for friendly territory and landed at Mons, Belgium, where we were able to pick up a wreck of a war weary aircraft and get back home. You could say I had a bit of a rough start to my tour.'

There is a rather bizarre story that needs telling even if only to show the camaraderie between the crews. Tech/Sgt Paul Kuchinski, Engineer/Top Turret Gunner takes up the story. 'Once while on a practise mission we were contacted by the Control Tower to assist a returning aircraft which had been shot up. It seems they had been badly mauled and among other things had lost their airspeed indicator, this being a vital piece of equipment. Without it you had no idea how fast you were going and, when you were trying to land, not to have one would have been the kiss of death. We were requested to fly just off their wing in order that we could lead them into a landing pattern and help them maintain proper airspeed while doing so. Anything below 110 mph would cause the aircraft to drop like a rock. When we caught up with the stricken ship as it was coming in on approach and I could see the damage, it makes you feel very indebted to the designer of the B-24 when you see how much stick it can take and still fly.

'The crew of the sick ship lived in our hut. It's a little bit nerve-racking when you see any ship in that state trying to do the impossible, but when they are friends it's even worse.

'I took up my usual position between the pilot and co-pilot, holding on to the backs of their seats. It was my job to call out the airspeed to the other aircraft and make him keep up with us so he could come in at the right speed. I am pleased to say that all went well and we got them down safely, but the one thing that really sticks in my mind is the sight of the waist gunner we used to call "Pappy", because he was in his thirties and we were all teenage kids. Anyway "Pappy" was standing at the waist window jumping and shouting, waving his arms about all the way down until we landed. Ben LePore was as usual very sedate and calm about the whole thing. To look at him you would think this was an everyday occurrence. Ben went on to finish his tour and returned home to Massachusetts. I don't recall what happened to "Pappy" but I think he made it.'

Paul tells another story of a time when they were returning from a mission to Berlin. 'They had taken some considerable damage from flak and were unable to keep up with the formation. They were lagging far behind and soon found themselves on their own. Knowing that they would be vulnerable to fighter attack they were very much on edge, but suddenly out of nowhere a P-47 appeared – he too had been damaged and was limping back. The pilot called up *Big Brother* (Paul's aircraft) and asked the pilot, Ralph Elliot, if he could slide under his wing and follow him home. Ralph addressed him as *Little Brother* and bade him welcome. Shortly a Me-109 came up on them, and although he was a mile or two away it was obvious he was going to attack the easy picking of a lame B-24. He was slightly higher than the B-24 and could not see the P-47 as he lined up for the attack. Ralph called up *Little Brother* and told him what was about to happen. The P-47 slid out from under our wing and made threatening movements and the Me-109 thought better of it and veered off.' Two sick planes had saved one another's skin.

Sgt Kuchinski tells of one of the most frightening stories of his time as an upper turret gunner. 'It was on our way back from a raid to Berlin; I can't remember the date, but I know I was nearing the end of my tour of duty. We had been warned to keep a lookout for unfamiliar allied aircraft. It seems the Germans had taken to putting up some of our captured planes into formation to mingle in with us and then to shoot us down using 20 mm cannon from the waist window. This caused a lot of tension. I did not see any of these, but on this particular trip we had just left the target when there were unusual flashes of light in the sky above us. Then suddenly I could hear gunfire and several of our guys started to fall out of the sky. Before I could clearly see what was happening the flashes had gone and the firing stopped. It seems that the Germans had jet aircraft that could stay airborne under power for twenty minutes. They would gain altitude above us, then swoop in firing at random and go straight through the formation. We lost quite a few ships that day. That was the only time I saw them, but several of the guys on future missions told the same story, so I know I did not dream it.'

Another story in the list of 'strange' events, concerns an aircraft known as *Bold Venture III*.

It was Christmas Day 1944, the 467th had flown a mission to bomb the railway centre at Mechernich, Germany. They had encountered very little trouble on the way, but there was very heavy flak over the target, inflicting considerable damage to a number of aircraft. As they left the target and turned for home they came up against the mighty Luftwaffe fighters. *Bold Venture* had been badly damaged by flak and was dropping out of formation, an ideal target for fighters. She was attacked several times by the fighters and was going down with gaping holes everywhere and two of her four engines out of action, one being on fire. 1st Lt Paul Ehrlich, *Bold Venture*'s pilot, sounded the alarm bell and the crew knew from this that it was time to get ready to bale out.

The Navigator and Bombardier, being in the nose of the aircraft, set to and removed their flak jackets and strapped on their 'chest chutes'. In doing so, they had to unplug their intercom system for a few minutes. On plugging it back in, they called up the pilot to tell him they were ready to jump on the order to do so but got no reply. They went up to the flight deck and found it empty. The pilot and co-pilot had already gone and so had most of the other crew. The order had been given while their intercom was disconnected, and they had not heard it. The Navigator checked their position and found they were still over enemy territory. They were unsure what to do. Should they bale out and stand a chance of being captured, or should they try to get as near to home as possible? They did not relish the idea of possibly being made prisoners of war so near to Christmas. The air pressure of the descending plane had extinguished the flames in the engine. They decided that as *Bold Venture* was still airborne they would set the automatic pilot to straight and level, hoping the aircraft would come down in the sea and not crash land on civilians. A 'Mustang' fighter plane on his way home spotted the stricken aircraft and decided to give them cover from further enemy attack. The remaining crew of the Liberator stayed with the aircraft for another thirty minutes until they were over friendly territory, then, much to the surprise of the Mustang, baled out. *Bold Venture*, still on automatic pilot, flew on and on, in fact *Bold Venture* flew all the way over the North Sea, over Britain, until eventually she ran out of fuel and started gently to glide towards the ground. The occupants of 'Lower House Farm', Vowchurch, near Hereford, were enjoying their festive relaxations when

[48]

suddenly they heard a very loud tearing noise from outside their door. On opening the front door they were confronted by a Liberator lying on its belly just yards away, with one of its engines embedded in a tree. The occupants of the house rushed out to attempt to help the crew, only to find the plane empty. Thinking the crew had been thrown clear, they made a search of the local area only to come back empty handed. The nearby RAF Station at Madley was informed and sent a mountain rescue team racing to the area with a view to finding injured crew members somewhere. Eventually they learned that the crew was safe and well in Belgium. The news that one of the group's aircraft had landed damaged, but fairly well intact, near Hereford, came as a great surprise to the men at 467 Group headquarters. A recovery team was dispatched with all haste to Vowchurch to assess the damage. Because of the nature of the ground and the fact that the road was nearby, they were able to salvage *Bold Venture III*. She was taken away under strict security and delivered to Watton.

As for the crew of *Bold Venture III*, those who baled out over Germany were captured and interned for the duration, with the exception of T/Sgt Frank C. Saunders. He was never found and listed MIA (missing in action). S/Sgt John V. Salen was injured during his descent, but he was picked up and hospitalised in Belgium where he made a full recovery.

There is an unusual story in a privately published book by Alan Healey written in 1946. It tells of a mission towards the end of the war. 'One of the rough missions was our last to Berlin on 18th March 1945. The target was a factory on the west side of the city. Accurate and intense flak began to burst among the ships of the lead squadron. Chapman's lead plane was hit and started down out of control. The deputy lead had only a few seconds to take over and make the bomb site and they dropped short of the target. A plane from the second squadron ran into and through the flak and dropped a perfect pattern on the industrial buildings. In the vertical picture taken by them you could see Chapman's plane going down. It was severely damaged. The navigator was killed by a hit in the head. The engineer had been blown to bits as he squatted to watch the bombs away. They lost four thousand feet. A large hole smashed in the plane's nose helped to put out a fire in the bomb bay. The Liberator was brought under control and, on two engines, headed straight across the city for the Russian lines forty miles away. An Me-109 was driven off by Russian Yak fighters which then proceeded to take passes at them. Only one engine was then pulling and they were losing twelve hundred feet a minute in altitude. They baled out beyond the lines and were shot at by the Yaks as they descended and then from the ground by Russian rifle-men. They were manhandled when they landed, but one of the crew could speak Polish and the Russians finally realised they were not German paratroopers but were "Ya Amerikanets". Then the vodka bottles came out and things were friendly. A funeral with full honours was given the navigator. They flew a war weary B-24 back through Italy to Rackheath in late April.'

The saddest story of the 467th took place on 29th December 1944. It is known in the history books as the 'Bears Grove' incident.

The group had been ordered to bomb Prum, Germany. The winter was unusually hard, hard that is for Norfolk. Heavy snow had fallen and on this particular day it was very foggy. This was known as 'Nil Sector Visibility', which meant an 'instrument take-off' as no one could see where they were going. The group was to be led by Lt Col Wallace, Sqn Com. to the 791st. Col Wallace was the first to make an attempt to take-off. Although he did manage to get airborne, in doing so he had clipped the trees, which were known as Bears Grove, at the end of the runway. His aircraft had received major damage from the impact and he fought desperately to gain control of the craft. At the same time he ordered his radio operator to report the problem and advise that the take-off should be aborted. He feared that some of the less experienced pilots were in danger of not getting off the ground. But he was too late.

The second aircraft was already thundering down the runway when the radio message was received. The plane was being flown by 2nd Lt Kurt F. Schellhas. The aircraft could not be seen on the runway due to the fog, but his engines were heard to go onto emergency power. Then a very loud crack was heard as the B-24 hit the trees at the end of the runway. Lt Schellhas's plane crashed in the field next to Wroxham railway bridge. As this was going on, a third aircraft attempted the take-off he too hit the trees, but did manage to stay airborne for a short period. He was forced to crash land at the nearby air base of Attlebridge.

A fourth aircraft also attempted the take-off. As these planes were taking off at between fifteen and thirty second intervals, it was not possible to get the message to the crews in time to tell them to abort. As a result the fourth plane, flown by 1st Lt David W. Foster, also hit the trees, and he too crashed at Wroxham railway bridge. In this case fate took a cruel hand in the outcome. As the first aircraft crashed at the bridge not all were killed, and the survivors were trying to extricate themselves from the plane when Lt Foster's plane landed directly on top of them. Sixteen men perished in this disaster. Parts and ammunition from these two aircraft are still being found today. As for Col Wallace's aircraft that had clipped the trees and been damaged, he flew his plane out to sea, baled out and he and his crew were picked up. The mission was aborted and no more 'Nil Sector' take-offs were ordered.

CHAPTER SIX

The Enemy Amongst Us

An entry in pilot Ralph Elliot's diary reads:
'8/15/44, fourth mission. Target, Vechta, Germany. Target for today was the Kanger area at Vechta, Germany, which lies south of Bremen and north of Dumber Lake. We took off at 0900 loaded with four 1,000 lb G.P. (general purpose) bombs and four 500 lb incendiary clusters. We crossed the North Sea and into Germany over the Friesian Islands and into the target which the formation hit dead centre. Only two of our bombs went out and the salvo handle wouldn't work at first so that we dumped six bombs in the town of Vechta itself. Saw a large fire after the explosion so we must have hit an oil dump accidentally. We must have raised hell with 1500 lbs of incendiaries in the town, as well as 3,000 lbs of TNT and steel. Aircraft H 42-52590 1,550 gallons of fuel used.'

In a later entry in the journal Ralph goes on to say: 'There was no more flak but the boys saw about twenty-five scare bombs near the target. They came up leaving a trail of white smoke and then exploded, but didn't seem to do any damage. The fun began just as we came back out and were nearly to the Zuider Zee. Fighters Ju-88s and Me-109s hit the formation just behind us and my boys saw four B-24s go down. A couple blew up and the other two spun out of control. The P-51s began chasing them and got some. A P-51 came up alongside and made the bad mistake of pointing his nose at us. My nose gunner Lt Parodi, top turret gunner Kuchinski and waist gunner Logan opened up on him as did some of the other ships, and my boys hit him, as we saw some smoke. Sorry, but he should have known better than that. The Germans have some captured equipment and have used our planes against us, so we had been told not to take any chances. The pursuit boys know we'll shoot and know better for the most part.

'This was similar to the way Warren Ewert got shot down. B-17 gunners disabled his P-51 and another burst jammed his canopy, so he had to make a dead stick landing in a German potato field and wait for the Germans to get him out. He was quite bitter about that even after the war.'

Tech/Sgt Paul Kuchinski, the top turret gunner who was said to be partly responsible for shooting down the P-51 takes up the story.

'It was as the Skipper said really, with the exception that I remember there were about eighty fighters coming at us from all directions. Our 51s were in full pursuit and scoring quite a few kills. We had been warned about the Krauts having some of our refurbished planes which were getting into the Squadron and shooting our guys down. This guy made a looping swerve at us, a sure sign he was lining up to attack, I was unsure if he was ours or a phoney, so I put a burst across his nose. He ignored the warning and kept coming. I could hear the Skipper and the Navigator screaming at me through my earphones to get the bastard. When you are in that situation, the noise, the shouting, someone trying to kill you, instinct takes over. So when I heard the Skipper screaming in my ear, I lined him up for another burst. Just then one of my two guns jammed, but I let rip with the other one. He was so close I couldn't miss. I racked him from his tail up the fuselage. I saw smoke and he flipped over and went down.

'We did not know until after we got back that it was one of ours. It seems that a 109 was underneath us and about to attack; the P-51 had spotted him and was coming in for the kill on him. But I got the P-51 first. As luck would have it another P-51 came in from the other side and took out the 109. He sure as hell saved our bacon. It's ironic when you think about it: if we had been in our normal ship, the bottom turret gunner would have spotted the Kraut plane, but the Boss decided we should have the new model aircraft. It didn't have a bottom turret; that was replaced by radar.

'I had to go before the Board of course and explain my actions. My crew backed me up, I told the truth and was cleared of blame. I learned only that the P-51 pilot was a major and that he got out of his aircraft OK but lost an arm in the process. I wanted to find him and apologise, but I was told to forget it. It affected me for years after the war, it still makes me emotional when I talk about it, even after all this time.'

The Germans had a fair array of patched up allied planes which they often put up when a formation of RAF or USAAF bombers came over. They tended to mingle in with the Allies and shoot them down.

When there was a large bomber stream made up from several groups, it was not unusual for some stragglers to lose their own squadron and slide into another group. Therefore one would often see a group of bombers together, all with different squadron or group markings. The Germans soon caught on to this and used it to full advantage.

Towards the end of 1944 the Germans were making one last desperate fling to regain control of the skies. Ralph Elliot wrote that on every trip more and more German fighters of all descriptions were coming at them.

From the way they flew it was obvious that not all the enemy pilots were experienced. The P-51s were accounting for quite a few of them, but they were not having it all their own way and were taking a fair few losses themselves. On one mission when the 467th was part of a bigger wing, the 445th bomb group lost thirty-two of thirty-six planes in the one mission. They were virtually wiped out in the space of about six minutes. The Eighth Air Force was to lose one hundred and ten bombers in four days. Fortunately this did not last for long; by this time the Allied fighters of all nations were freely available and made short shrift of this last ditch effort by Vice Reichmarshall Chancellor Herman Göring's mighty Luftwaffe.

Tech/Sgt Paul Kuchinski tells of the incident when his plane was called to help down a crew who had their instruments shot away.

The damaged aircraft was known as *Mardobea* (the name was made up of the officer's wives, Marlyn, Dorothy and Bea). It was 21st November 1944, *Mardobea* was on a mission to Hamburg and the pilot was 1st Lt Robert E. Feldtkeller. They had just started their bomb run and the sky was full of heavy and accurate flak. One shell exploded only five feet below the wing of the aircraft, shrapnel from the shell sprayed the Liberator, one engine caught fire and the bomber began to lose speed and altitude. Lt Feldtkeller kept the aircraft level until the bombs were dropped on the target.

Turning away from the target and heading for home, Lt Feldtkeller and his crew began assessing the damage. They found that all the engine instruments, navigational instruments and hydraulic systems and all but one of the radio frequencies had been shot away and they later counted one hundred and forty-two shrapnel holes in the aircraft, but not one of the crew received anything more than a few minor scratches.

As *Mardobea* headed for home, they soon found they had no real means of navigation and they knew they were an ideal target for fighters. Lt Feldtkeller ordered every man to keep his eyes peeled, while he tried to think of how they were going to get back to base. As luck would have it Lt Jerome K. Dapper, navigator, always carried a small pocket compass which he primarily used to find his way back to base when he was out on trips around the Norfolk countryside during his time off. Remember that in wartime the road signs had been removed. With the aid of this pocket compass Lt Dapper worked out the general direction of England but finding the base was an entirely different matter. All the crew carried very small compasses in their escape kit but these would have been useless in attempting to guide the plane home. They were not subject to fighter attack, in fact they did not see even one. Eventually they reached the North Sea and were somewhat surprised when the English coast came into view. Crossing the coast, they called for assistance. Eventually they contacted Rackheath tower and explained their predicament and asked that *Little Pete* be sent to meet them, but the tower did not seem to understand their plight fully because they simply said *Little Pete* was not in the air. After much cursing from the Radio Operator the tower at last grasped the seriousness of the situation and said they would send help.

Mardobea was picked up by Paul Kuchinski's crew and was guided back to the base. When they came to let the undercarriage down, they found that the hydraulic fluid had drained out of the landing gear. The two planes circled the field so an attempt could be made to lower the undercarriage by hand. This was a long job and *Mardobea* was running very short of fuel, but they continued to circle until at last the wheels were locked down. The two planes landed safely, but it was touch and go for a while.

A Bomber crew
(l. to r.) standing: Lts Parodi, Yukovich, Elliot (pilot), Moser, Thompson
kneeling: Sgts Ulman, Logan, Meagher, Kuchinski, Simoff, Fritsch

CHAPTER SEVEN

'Crew, Bale Out'

A s in all theatres of war, not all are going to return to their homeland. This was no less true of some of the men of the 467th.

Some, when they were shot down, were lucky enough to bale out safely and be made prisoners of war. If you can call being interned for the duration lucky, but at least they were alive and, given the circumstances, in reasonably good health. There were a few who managed to evade capture and return home via the Dutch and French underground, but they were the exception rather than the rule.

Many believe, with the help of films and books, that a crew who were shot down, just jumped out of the aircraft, landed, contacted the underground and were whisked off back home. Sadly this was far from the truth.

The worst scenario one can imagine, apart from not being able to get out at all, is to bale out, land safely, only to be executed or murdered by the enemy. Such was just the case of the crew of *Osage Express*. It was 21st June 1944. The groups sixtieth mission was to bomb the workshops at Genshagen, Berlin.

The pilot, 1st Lt Edwin M. Helton and his crew from the 790th squadron, took severe flak damage over Berlin. They managed to continue their flight, bomb the target and turn for home. Lt Helton joined the reassembled formation on the homeward trip, but their damage was too severe. They tried to stay with the group, but began to struggle and drop out of the pattern. The aircraft was last seen falling back, but Lt Helton seemed to be still in control. One can only guess at what stage he gave the order to abandon the aircraft, but they all managed to bale out successfully. They landed safely but were captured by the SS who promptly murdered them on the spot.

Two months later, on 5th August 1944, 2nd Lt Willard A. Langenfeld and his crew were on the group's ninety-first mission. Their target was a factory and airfield at Brunswick, Germany. The formation had gone in and bombed the target and was in the process of turning for home. The flak on this particular day was very intense and several of the planes were hit and did not make it back.

Lt Langenfeld's plane was among them. He had taken a lot of punishment. He knew they were not going to get home, but he attempted to get as near to the coast as he could. He only managed a short distance when it became obvious that the aircraft was in danger of blowing up or disintegrating, so he ordered the crew to bale out. They all evacuated safely and found themselves coming down near the town of Minden. Once on the ground, they were immediately set upon by hostile German civilians. Seven of the crew were killed by the incensed mob before the German Army could arrive. Lt Langenfeld, 2nd Lt Charles E. Whiteacre (co-pilot) and Staff Sergeant John A. Vititoe (Ball Turret Gunner) were rescued by the Army and made prisoners of war.

Some crews were able to evade capture and internment. 1st Lt Bill F. Moore and his crew from the 788th were lead ship on 29th April 1944. Because they were lead ship, they had an extra passenger in the shape of Major Robert L. Salzarulo. The Major was command pilot for this trip. The group bombardier, a Lt Low, was also on board at the time.

Their mission was to bomb Friedrichstrasse Station in Berlin (the 'Big B' as it was known). They had turned into the target area through a hail of flak and heavy cloud. The German ack-ack gunners were hitting them hard. With the cloud cover so thick, they could only find the south side of the city so they readjusted the target to the Tempelhof district.

Lt Moore's plane, having bombed the target, was hit when it came out the other side. He did not seem to be too badly damaged and turned for home. He was struggling to keep up with the homeward formation, but pressed onward. It was not until he was over Holland that he realised they were desperately short of fuel and they must have taken damage to the fuel tanks or lines. To add to their troubles the engines became very erratic and started to overheat. It was obvious to Lt Moore and the crew that they were not going to make it home. The order was given to bale out. The entire crew, including Lt Moore, got clear of the aircraft and landed safely. They were quite spread out by the time they reached the ground, so they attempted to link up with one another, while at the same time trying to evade German patrols.

The Germans however had seen them jump and were searching the area where it was thought they would land. Five of the crew were captured, including Major Salzarulo and Lt Moore. The other five did manage to evade the Germans and were later picked up by the Dutch underground, who were able to spirit them away and eventually return them to England.

The following is an extract from a diary of an unnamed member of another crew who took part in that raid. 'Our flak damaged ships developed trouble coming back, with engines out and props feathered, they struggled towards the Zuider Zee. Enemy fighters were after the lagging planes. Three of ours went down. One of these had Major Salzarulo as command pilot and its bombardier was Lt Low, the group bombardier. They were last heard saying they had to abandon ship, much later we learned that many of the thirty-two who went down that day were prisoners. We did not hear of Lt Low.

'Nearly a year later he came back. He told us of his jump, how he opened his "chute" immediately because he was anxious to see if it worked. He had landed safely and had been hidden by the Dutch underground. Disruption of the French railways had kept him in Holland. He spent a month in a cave and other long periods in straw stacks, being moved around at frequent intervals. Some time later he had been with fifty other US and RAF flyers trying to cross the Rhine after the Allied breakthrough. They were being led by the underground and barely escaped when they stumbled on the Germans who had moved into that area a couple of days previously. A large number of men were killed. At some stage he had hidden in a secret wall compartment and a prodding German had put his bayonet into the only 2x4 in the wall and this saved him from discovery. We were glad to see him that next spring.

As to the plight of the captured men, they were made prisoners of war and all were interned for the duration with the exception of Lt Moore. He was handed over to the Gestapo though no reason for this has ever been found, and who eventually executed him at King William III Barracks in December 1944.

Most of the planes fell victim to flak damage as opposed to fighters, although fighters did account for a large number of aircraft. Baling out of a Liberator was not always as easy as it sounds. There can be nothing more terrifying than being in an aircraft you know is going down and for one reason or another cannot get out.

2nd Lt David E. Love and his crew were flying *Perils of Pauline* when they received severe flak damage over the target. Lt Love made a valiant effort to return home, but his aircraft was so badly damaged that they dropped out of formation and it was obvious to all that the plane could not sustain flight for much longer. Finally the aircraft went into a flat spin and Lt Love ordered the crew to bale out. Because of the rate of descent and the centrifugal force of the spinning aircraft, evacuation was virtually impossible.

Lt Love managed to get out safely. The co-pilot jumped clear, but because of the urgency of getting out quickly, he had not buckled his parachute up tight enough and he fell out of his chute. Needless to say he lost his life.

The Radio Operator was going out through the bomb bay, but he too fell out before he could secure his parachute – remember this plane was spinning out of control. The Bombardier baled out only to hit the propeller when he was caught in the slip stream and was killed. The engineer/top turret gunner did get clear and landed safely.

The rest of the crew went down with the ship. Lt Love and the engineer were captured and made prisoners of war. In all eight men lost their lives that day in just one aircraft. When a plane goes into a flat spin, the centrifugal force pins the crew into their positions and they are unable to move. Knowing the plane is going to crash, the fear must be beyond belief.

Those who did manage to get out were far from safe. Many died for various reasons: parachutes not opening properly; falling out of a chute; being hit by the aircraft or being murdered when they reached the ground. A few were lucky and, although they were captured, they were treated reasonably well and were able to return home at the end of the hostilities.

Crew of *Perils of Pauline* (left to right):
M. Deutsch (Nav), R. Sander (C.P.), E. Beaney (Pilot), W. Davis (Bomb),
R. Finch (Ball Gnr/3rd Eng), B. Meredith (Tail Gnr), V. Peveauet (Radioman),
R. Rainwater (1st Eng), C. Kleinert (R.Waist/2nd Eng), G. Leeper (Nose Turret)

CHAPTER EIGHT

A Pilot's Life

Life for the average pilot was not all beer and skittles as many books and films would have us believe. He is just your ordinary Joe, over here, miles from home and his loved ones. He just wants to get on with his job, do his tour of missions safely and quickly and get back home as soon as he can. This is his story.

'Being awakened in the middle of the night by the squadron watch officer and told it's 0200 hrs is not the best of starts to any day. You have slept, but very badly. You never get used to going on a mission, no matter how many you have done. The first few are not too bad, you are more in fear of doing what you have trained to do rather than fear of what can happen. It's when you get to about ten or twelve missions, that you tend to become 'Flak Happy'. This has been described by the medics as fifty per cent fatigue and fifty per cent pure fear; the stage when you know what you have got to do and the fear of knowing what can happen takes over. The stomach starts to churn, you wish you had not had supper last night. You make a fast dive for the latrines, you just want to crawl back into bed and sleep for a week. But you shake yourself out of it and start to think about the job in hand. Where will it be today? A milk run would be nice, but you know that it is unlikely. In your heart you know that that metal monster they call a B-24 has been sitting out there all night just dreaming of ways to kill you. The strange thing is, you have a love-hate relationship with your aircraft. You hate it because you know it is trying to kill you; not the Germans, your damned aeroplane. But at the same time you love it; it will take you off to God knows where and it is so reliable; it will bring you home again.

'Ablutions are very important prior to going on a mission, not so much for being clean and tidy (like my mom always says "what happens if you get knocked down and you haven't got clean underwear on"), no, it's more that having to wear an oxygen mask for several hours tends to irritate over stubble, so a shave is of utmost importance, even if it is in cold water.

Ready for action

'If you are a lead crew you would have to attend a pre-briefing, which was held about one hour before the main briefing. At the pre-brief the maps would all be marked out with the route etc. and the operations officer, duty navigator and intelligence officers would be on hand to give any special features of the mission. You had a good idea what to look out for. Flak and fighters, they are always there. The stomach is beginning to settle now but another quick trip to the latrines does not go amiss.

'After a pre-brief, it is breakfast time. You don't feel much like eating, but you know you must. It could be a long time before you eat again and at least you knew it would be real eggs and not that powdered stuff they serve up when you are not flying. After breakfast it's on to the main brief and by this time all the relevant crew members are there. You nod to a few, you mumble a few words to others, but you don't really want to talk. If the target is Hamm or Ruhr you know you are in for a bad one. The Ruhr Valley was known as Flak Alley. It would be just your luck to draw that one. Here we get all the usual stuff. The board, when the curtain is drawn back, shows the target. You might hear a few groans when the rest of the crews see it. A blood red ribbon shows the route across and a pink one shows the return route, not always the same way in as the way out. I always thought that to be odd, showing a blood red ribbon as the path to possible death and destruction and I wonder if it was some sort of sick joke (more likely that the numskull, who put it up, never had a brain to think with). The radio operator gets his call signs and the colours of the day and fuse settings are also discussed. Then a pep talk from Col Shower or one of his aides and at the end of briefing the Chaplain gives a few words of comfort. It's all right for him, he's not going. If you want to say a prayer with him, a small room has been set aside. I have seen many a man, who would curse and blind at anyone, become humble and seek the solace of prayer before a mission. This was not thought by anyone to be a sign of weakness. I have done it myself on more than one occasion. Then it's attention while staff officers leave, and then we are dismissed.

'Next come the medics to diagnose any ailments and dish out anti-doze pills and nose drops. The thought runs through your mind that you would come up with some ailment or other to avoid going on this one, but then you dismiss it. If you go on this one, it's one nearer to the completion of your tour.

'After all the instructions in the field orders have been carried out, you pick up your kit and your escape kit, which would comprise a silk map, a silly little compass, a small photo of you in civilian clothes so if the underground pick you up they can make papers for you with your photo, some money and some glucose sweets. Then it's out to the trucks that take you to the aircraft, You then have roughly half an hour to do the pre-flight checks. This starts with walking round the aircraft to see if there are any visible signs of damage including tyre damage. The last thing you want is a blow out on take-off when you are loaded with bombs. By this time the engineer and ground crew have pulled through the props at least six times. The engineer would also check you have the right amount of fuel and the oil is topped up and Radio Ops would check to see if his radio is in fine working order. At this stage, you still have an uncomfortable feeling in the pit of your stomach, but your mind is focused on making sure this aircraft is going to get you there, and more to the point, get you home.

'We had previously dressed in our flying suits back in the dressing room, and, depending on the time of the year, it was usually long johns, heated flying suits (make sure they work), outer fur covering and heavy heated boots. On our hands we wear silk gloves followed by fur mittens, as 20,000 feet was about ten or fifteen below freezing. Thinking back, we looked like robots because with all that gear we could hardly move. Some even tied their low shoes around their waist in case they baled out and had to walk. We would normally finish dressing just before we boarded the aircraft. This usually meant putting on flak jackets, Mae Wests etc. Ten minutes to go, just time for a last cigarette and a final chance to relieve yourself, either behind the ground crew hut or against one of the aircraft wheels, then time to climb aboard. Take-off is getting close now, the stomach starts to rumble and you wish you had visited the latrines again. Cockpit checks, intercom and radio checks, get a report from the rest of the crew, making sure all is well at their particular station. Start the engines, run them for a while, check all pressures and dials. All is well, sign the release form from the ground crew to say the aircraft is fit for duty. I wish I had gone to the latrines before I got into this damned plane.

'Sit back and wait for the yellow flare; that's our signal to taxi, watch out for your pre-determined slot in the bomber stream. Now the engines are run up again, making sure the magnetos do not drop below 100 rpm. Check take-off clearances, set the gyros with the runway heading and we are off, thundering down the runway. Is this thing going to lift off when I ask it to? The co-pilot calls out the speed: "sixty, seventy, eighty, ninety, one hundred and ten", we are airborne. The sweat runs down my face, I can feel my hair damp not from exertion, you understand, but the fear of us not lifting off and running out of runway with a full bomb load. You can hear the sigh of relief from the crew when we lift off. They too have the same fear.

'Wheels up, flaps up, reduce power settings and keep checking the dials and temperature gauges. Climbing at about 300 ft a minute now and turning to the radio beacon at Cromer. After reaching about 5,000 we turn left

Over Caister Flats

on to a heading of 210° magnetic. Stomach settled again, I can hear the chatter from the crew over the intercom. Still we climb and turn every 2,000 ft to stay in our own air space at 10,000 ft, I instruct the crew to go on oxygen. When we reach between 13,000 and 15,000 ft, depending on the assembly altitude for the day, we keep a look out for "Big Pete", the "Judas Goat" as we called him. After we get into our assigned slot, the group moves off to join the other groups of the wing. Sometimes, if the wing is a thousand bomber force, the stream of aircraft would be thirty miles or more long. It has been known for the first section to be over the target when the last section is just leaving the English coast. I can hear the co-pilot checking the crew about every fifteen minutes over the intercom. His monotonous tones sound in my ear, "Pilot to crew, oxygen check" and they would answer back "Nose OK, Navigator OK, Radio OK," and so on and this would go on until we were well over the sea.

'Every time I see the English coast slide away underneath me, I cannot help wondering if I am ever going to see it again. Out over the North Sea the gunners check their guns, just a short burst you understand, they only have 500 rounds to each gun and we might need every one of those. A Browning clears 500 rounds in a minute so it doesn't take a genius to work out how much fire power we have. Because it's so cold at altitude I know one of the gunners used to put a round in before take-off. He used to say that because it was so cold, his guns froze and he could not load them up in the air. When he fired his one round the heat would unfreeze the guns enabling him to load up. This was against the rules, but what the hell, so long as he was careful and didn't shoot the tail off on take-off, I just looked the other way.

'Soon we are heading for the target, still listening for the word "Dike", that would be our recall sign if the mission was called off. Every man is keeping his eyes open for enemy fighters. As soon as we cross the enemy coast, the flak starts coming up to meet us. That's something else you cannot get used to; it still puts the fear of God into you. It's even worse for the new pilots and crews who have never experienced it before. When the shells explode you can hear small pieces of shrapnel hitting the fuselage and it sounds like a shower of rain hitting a corrugated tin roof. You just hope it is far enough away not to do you any damage. I did hear a story of two guys from another ship coming to blows at 20,000 ft. It seems the one was sitting on an ammunition box when he accused another of the guys of kicking him very hard in the butt. They started to argue and then blows were thrown. Can you imagine it, two guys trying to fight at 20,000 ft clothed in their full flying suits. You have a job to walk, let alone fight. The upshot seems to have been that the guy sitting on the ammunition box did get a good thump in the butt, but it was from a piece of shrapnel that had gone through the fuselage, through the ammunition box and hit very hard at his flak jacket which he was sitting on. He was one lucky guy, but the pilot had a great deal of trouble settling these guys down. The only consolation is, that if you have flak, you are unlikely to get fighters on your tail. On the coast and inland the flak is sometimes very light, but it still worries me. I keep thinking that these boys are counting on me to get them through this safely and get them home; it puts an extra strain on the mind. No wonder they say we look old before our time.

'The flak stops, we all know what that means – fighters. They come screaming in so fast it is difficult for the gunners to know where to shoot. I can hear them over the intercom shouting warnings to one another and the guns firing. It would usually be the top turret gunner shouting the warnings as he had better vision than anyone else. To assist him define left from right in the heat of the moment, we had a figure nine painted on the cowling of number three engine and a figure three painted on the starboard outer. This enabled him to call out the fighter position using the "clock" position. The noise and vibration is tremendous. Sometimes there are so many fighters that it seems they cannot fail to shoot us down. But we survive. Sometimes we take some damage but we still keep flying. The worst part is when you see the plane in front or at the side of you go down. We all keep one eye on it to see if we can see any "chutes" while keeping the other eye on what we are supposed to be doing. It's always sad when it happens, especially if it is someone you know, but secretly we are all a little bit pleased it was them and not us. But we knew it could be us at any moment. In the early days, we didn't have any of our fighters for protection. They couldn't reach deep into Europe. This was to change in the later stages when we had P-51 Mustangs, which would cover us all the way to the target.

'At last we turn in for the target run and it seems like we have been flying for ever. If you have gone to "Flak Alley", all you can see is a big black cloud dancing around in front of you. You know this is an "iron cloud" – a wall of flak which you feel there is no way through. But you go on, you fly straight for it, and hope and pray it doesn't get you. You're not really scared at this point because your training takes over. You know what you have to do. You just do it: the fear returns later.

'At the I.P. (Initial Point) the lead aircraft fires his yellow flares, a sign for the bomb run to begin. Now it's straight and level flying, no deviation from the course or altitude, no matter what happens until the bombs are away. This is usually about eighteen to twenty minutes, but it seems a lot longer. The lead ship fires a red flare, we open the bomb bay doors and on down the bomb run we fly, every one tucked in tight to get a good bomb pattern. The navigator is in the nose watching for the lead ship to send out his smoke marker. By this time the bombardier is glued to his bomb sight. You are waiting for his instruction, waiting for his call "Bombs Away", waiting for what seems an eternity. You know the rest of the crew are willing him to press the bomb release and say the magic words, and all the time you are being buffeted and thrown around as flak continues to burst around you. You might hear a half silent prayer from somewhere in the ship.

'At last the bombardier lets go of your cargo, the Radio Operator checks that the bomb bay is empty and that none have hung up. Now close the bomb bay doors and make a steady left hand turn away from the target and head for home. You may see two or three more of your comrades going down at this time, but you cannot help but feel relief. You have made it so far and all you want to do is get home. But you know it's not the end. You still have the fighters and flak on the way home, though you know you will meet up with you own fighters somewhere on the way. They will give you protection, but that is a long way off yet. Keep turning, look for the lead ship, get into formation as quick as you can, you know it's your only chance of surviving.

'You call for a crew check; each member of the crew calls he is OK or perhaps one has been injured from shrapnel. You can only give him the briefest of attention at this stage. You are still in grave danger of flak or fighters and every man is needed to keep a sharp eye out. Other aircraft are heading for home around you and you try to stay in tight formation as this is the best protection you can have against fighters. You run the gauntlet of fighters and ground fire as you will this monster back towards the safety zone as fast as it can go. At last you meet your own fighters, coming to shepherd you home and you feel a little bit better now. If you have injured men aboard you can give them a little bit more attention, but the flight still seems never ending. You slip across the North Sea. If your ship has been hit you hope it will at least get you back onto dry land. The last place you want to go down is in the sea. You haven't much chance if you do, it's almost certainly a watery grave.

'The English coast appears, you feel the tension in the aircraft ease and you pick up the splashier beacon and head for base. Those that have injured on board have gone ahead by the shortest route and will be given priority landing, but the rest of us will stay in formation and pass right over the base. Those who took off first, will land first for obvious reasons, low on fuel. When it came to our turn to land, it was a quick pass over the control tower, who would give us the low down on whether we had sustained damage to our underside which we, of course, could not see. If all was clear, we would come into land.

'Touchdown is the oddest moment of the entire trip, all the pent up emotions are released in one instant. Prior to this, on approach, the crew had been fairly quiet, but now they start chattering like a truck load of monkeys. The things they talk about would give the casual observer the impression that the mission never took place, so relieved were they to get home in one piece. Every time I touched down, I had the greatest urge to pee. It somehow never occurred to me in flight, it was just when I put the ship down it came over me all of sudden.

'Taxiing round the perimeter to park at our allotted dispersal point, I had to get the engineer to sit on top of the aircraft to give me directions as to how close I was to any obstacle or other aircraft. The Liberator was built in such a way that I could not see the wing tips from the cockpit and it would have been easy to slice into another aircraft with my wing if I was not careful.

'Park the aircraft, shut down the engines, remember to leave brakes off, sign form no. 1 and make a note of any discrepancies and climb down on to mother earth once more. The ground engineer gives a big smile of relief that his crew and ship are home. The trucks would be waiting to take us to debriefing, but before I could get on the truck it was a quick relief behind the crew shack. Back at control, the first job was to hand in our escape kits and parachutes and stow our flying gear in our lockers. Coffee and sandwiches would be handed out by the Red Cross and then finally it was into the interrogation room. This was the same room we had received our briefing report in what seemed like an eternity ago.

'During the debrief, which was by way of a four page questionnaire supplied by S-2 officers (or sometimes it would be a meeting with an intelligence officer like old Egolf), we were given a shot of whisky by the medics. Apart from the gunners, who had to clean and store their guns, the rest of the crew were finished for the day. Officers, however, had to attend a discussion on the mission after first having a wash and brush up and perhaps a meal. That was my day done. The crew and I had completed another mission, one more towards the magic number. Then you try to forget all about it, maybe go back to your hut to write a letter to the wife telling her that you had a quiet day with nothing to report and then try to get some sack in. The only problem is, we have to go through it all again tomorrow or the next day. Will we be so lucky the next time?'

A pall of smoke rises from a bombing raid

CHAPTER NINE

Rest and Recreation

Life for the men of the 467th had a lighter side, with events to relieve the stresses and strains of war. The social activities on the base were very well organised. There was, of course, the inevitable bar and the Red Cross club where various functions were laid on, including local theatre groups coming in to perform the current popular plays and shows of the day. A group of boys even organised themselves into a band which went under the name of the 'Airliners', and about once a month the Red Cross would lay on a dance with the 'Airliners' doing the honours. Several of the locals enjoyed the music and the genial hospitality of the 467th. On odd occasions more well known bands would be invited to supply the music for the dance.

Considering the base was so close to Norwich, the recreational facilities were more than adequate. Sir Edward had made his tennis courts available to the men and its seems some quite fierce tournaments went on between the squadrons. Many were introduced to the game of cricket, although none felt compelled to take up the game as a career after the war. Baseball and soccer seemed the favourite pastimes apart, that is, from sampling huge quantities of local English beer. It was quite unlike the beer at home and many took a great liking to it.

There was of course a Liberty Bus or truck into Norwich each night and it seems that most of the men took advantage of the city night life at some time or other. The Samson and Hercules was their favourite spot. This place was affectionately known as 'Muscle Palace' but no one seems to know if this referred to the statues of the mighty strong men that adorn the entrance, or if it referred to the constant fights that took place within its portals. 'Muscle Palace' was the meeting point for all the American service men stationed on the various bases in Norfolk at the time, so of course it attracted many of the local girls, a fact which the local lads were not at all happy about. I fear it was because of this that many of the fights started. The local and Military Police were in constant attendance on dance nights.

The 'Airliners'

'R & R'

One crew member recalls his visit to 'Muscle Palace', 'You soon learnt from the guys who had been here a while that the place to find the girls on a Saturday night was at the Samson Ballroom. But you had to be able to defend yourselves, because many of the local guys took exception to us homing in on their girls, not that they seemed to be of real beauty, not like the drugstore beauties back home. They also seemed to be shabbily dressed and it took some time for us to realise these girls had to make do with whatever they could find as clothing was in short supply. It's amazing what they did come up with, often totally out of nothing. But as time went by we began to appreciate their country beauty and had some great times, in between the fights with the local guys that is. About once a month we had dances on the base and a lot of these girls were trucked in. They were trucked home again afterwards, or most of them were, though some were our guests for the night, providing the MPs didn't catch us. Make no mistake, we liked the local girls, why some of the guys even married them, but there were some who just supplied comforts to these young boys who were a long way from home. Needless to say they were very, very popular.'

For many the Liberty Bus returned from Norwich too early in the evening for their liking. The base curfew was not until midnight, so a bicycle was the favourite mode of transport, usually without lights of course, much to the consternation of the local constabulary. But the trusty bike was used on an array of sorties by the 467th, one of its favourite uses being as a means of touring the lanes around Norfolk. One air crew remembers, 'There was nothing more relaxing than cycling around the lanes on a bright summer's day. We would explore the lanes of Woodbastwick, Coltishall, Wroxham and Spixworth to name but a few. Everywhere was so green and peaceful, with hedges that must have taken centuries to grow, not like we were used to back home, just fences everywhere. You just wanted to lose yourself in the tranquillity of it all, particularly if you had done a rough mission the day before. Don't forget, we had spent months in the desert doing our training with nothing but sand and flies. To come to this, it was like heaven.'

A senior officer, remembers the spring and summer months in particular. 'Sometimes it was hard to remember what we were here for and that we were fighting a war. Everywhere was so peaceful. In the early morning the pheasants would be calling and the summer mist would be rising and you really felt good. By the same token, in the evening you would see rabbits playing – they were unafraid of us, or so it seemed. We were under strict orders not to hunt the game, but I have got to admit there were quite a few roast pheasant meals and the rabbit stew went down well. I remember too, when a V-2 landed just the other side of the road from the gate, it

Norwich in War

Non-motorised transport

landed in a field full of cows and quite a few were killed by the blast. Boy, were the beef steaks good! There were many birds new to us of course. I seemed to remember the robin being always around us. It seems silly now, but I am sure one robin used to follow me around. Everywhere I went he seemed to be there, maybe because I always talked to him. That bird took the brunt of many of my problems, but he was always happy to listen. The sounds of the blackbird and thrush were so sweet and clear, it made you feel at one with God. Peace was on the side of Rackheath, that is until the still air was shattered by the spluttering and roaring of B-24 engines. Then you came back to reality with a bang.'

One or two found watering holes other than the Samson and Hercules, when out on their trusty steeds. Top Turret Gunner/Engineer Paul Kuchinski recalls the nights he, as a nineteen year old, went on a 'Pubbing Mission' to the Brickmakers Arms in Sprowston. 'That place became like a second home to me. I met a lot of lovely people and learned to play the dreaded game of darts, dreaded because when you are learning it can cost you quite a lot of money. The rules were, if you lost a game, you were required to buy your opponent a drink. Well, needless to say, I lost quite a few games in the beginning; so much so that I thought I had better get proficient at this game before I went broke. Eventually I got the hang of it of course and didn't have to buy so many beers. In fact, in the end I was getting a few back. I did learn one other very important message during my nights at the Brickmakers, and that was to be sure and drink your own beer and not anyone else's. I remember I picked up my beer one night and took a big mouthful, I was feeling rather pleased with myself having just beaten one of the good players in the pub, when I began to seriously choke on a cocktail stick. It seems that a guy called "Sherlock" (I am sure that was a nickname), used to mark his drinks that way and I had unknowingly picked up his drink instead of my own. That was a lesson I never forgot.

'I had a great time there. Every time I went in I would give George the bartender a fixed amount of money and he would deduct the price of drinks when I bought them. Some nights it would not last long, depending on how many games of darts I lost. When it was all gone I would take my leave and head back to base, but not before getting fish and chips wrapped in newspaper. I always kept some dough in my sock for emergencies.

'As I got better at the game, my funds lasted all evening until Bill the proprietor shouted, "Time gentlemen please" and some nights I even had a refund. I figured, if I gave George a fixed amount of cash when I went in, I could eke out my funds until next pay-day. That way I would not have any dry "pubbing missions".

'I remember one night we had an air raid warning and we all had to leave the pub. Bill also owned a candy store across the road and he took me back there this night, I don't know, I guess he felt sorry for me, being a young lad far from home. Anyway we sat drinking beer and eating his delicious pickled onions – boy, were they sweet! We sat talking about something and nothing till the all clear sounded and by then it was time I got back to base. We said goodnight and Bill said we must do it again. Well, sure enough, going back to Bill's for after hours drinking became a regular thing. I could not get enough of his pickled onions! The only drawback was, I did take some serious flak from the guys in the plane the next day. Like I said, the place became a second home to me and I had some great times there. I even became the unofficial bouncer. When we had some loud mouthed Yanks in or some that got out of hand, I would throw them out, much to the amusement of the folk in there. I always said I could not stand noisy or troublesome Yanks.

'If we had been told we had an early call the next day, which usually meant a mission to the "Big B", we tended to stay on base and play cards, a game called "Hearts" as I remember. Going out pubbing the night before an early call was not a wise thing to do. You needed to keep your mind alert the next day, that is if you wanted to survive.

'Cycle racing became a favourite pastime when we were on the base. We were issued with English bikes, a lot lighter than ours with the brakes on the handlebars. Many went ass over bandbox when they gave that old front brake a bit too much of a squeeze, especially on the rough "Burma Road" through the dell to the Ops Block. Many a bent and buckled wheel was found there and many cuts and bruises were the result of too tight "flying".

One night, coming back from a pubbing mission on my trusty bike, I got on to the base OK, but as I had partaken of more than my fair share of beer, somewhere along the line the sidewalk jumped out to meet me. It threw me off my bike and I guess I must have been knocked out. When I came to I was in the infirmary. The MPs had picked me up and signed me in as a "pub mission" casualty of war. The next morning the guy in the next bed gave me hell. I had apparently woken up in the night shouting and hollering that I was blind. My bandage had slipped down over my eyes and I had thought the worst.

'One thing I do remember about my pubbing missions is that I had become friends with one of the MPs at the guard house. He was known as "Popeye", I don't know why. I remember he was small in stature but had a big heart. Anyway, I always used to bring him back two bottles of beer after each pubbing mission, just to keep him sweet, so that he would not report me to the officer of the day if I was a bit the worse for wear. On my way to the next mission to the Brickmakers, I would pick up the two empty bottles for a refill on my return. The system worked well and at no time did I get to be "front and centre" for being "D and D". I do remember whilst talking to him one night we heard some of the guys crashing through the woods on the way back to their huts and it was clear they had had a bit too much of the good old English beer. Anyway, Popeye shouted at them then fired a round into the woods and all went quiet. I asked him if he was going to see if he had hit anybody but he said no, they had gone quiet and that's all he wanted. There were no reports in the morning of anybody being found shot, so I guess he missed. I do remember my one and only frightening pub mission. I had decided to give the Brickmakers a miss and venture further into Norwich, but by the time I had got down the road a piece, I was tired of cycling and realised I was missing out on valuable drinking time, so at the next turn I turned left. I remember it was uphill and thought it was a silly move to make, when I came across several pubs. I dived into the first one and ordered a pint. While waiting for my drink I looked around and was surprised to see the place full of black GIs. A Sergeant wandered over to me and asked me what I thought I was doing (you must remember in those days we were segregated from the black guys and were not allowed to mix with them). When I saw all these guys I thought I was in for a good beating. I hastily explained my predicament to the sergeant. He paid for my drink and told me to drink up and leave quickly if I didn't want trouble. I drank very fast and beat a hasty retreat, lucky to come out in one piece. I did not venture from the Brickmakers again.'

About once a month, several of the men would get weekend passes to London. Rufus Webb, a waist gunner, remembers his trips.

'The first thing that struck me was the devastation and carnage every-where, but if you saw the inhabitants, you would think bombing was an everyday event in their lives. They seemed to take it all in their stride and they were so friendly towards us. We had the greatest respect for the people of London. One of the many things I remember is that at night everything was so black, not a light to be seen anywhere. It made getting around a bit difficult, but with the help of cabbies and the locals we found our way. The daytime was not much better either. All the stores had their windows covered with some form of dark coverings, so there was no colour anywhere, which was a stark contrast to the beautiful green of Norfolk. So my memory of London was a dark, grey, dreary and foggy city, but with lovely people.

'The first thing we did when we hit London was to have a nice long hot bath and a haircut. Then we would go off to the theatre to see a show or play. We never ever went to the movies. My crew and I always went every-where together, the NCOs that is. There were about six of us and I was the youngest at nineteen, so they all seemed to watch out for me, never letting me get into trouble. We stayed overnight in a servicemen's place, kinda like our YMCA. I think we all enjoyed the feeling of clean white linen sheets instead of woollen blankets we had back at base. Fish and chips spring to mind, we ate lots of those, they were so good. I guess the newspaper gave them that good taste, but I have never eaten them since.

'We did the usual things, visit the historical places like Westminster Abbey, Madame Tussauds and rode the subway, I think you call it the tube, can't think why. We did visit a pub or two, but I was not impressed with English beer, I am sure it was watered down. I know several of the other guys took pleasure in the seamier side of the night life, but that never appealed to me. I was too young and innocent to be bothered with such things and besides I had got a sweetheart waiting for me back home.'

Rufus was right. Many of the men did enjoy the night life. A Top Turret Gunner well remembers his visits to London for different reasons.

'Apart from Piccadilly and the surrounding area, we never did go for the usual stuff in London. We checked into the Rainbow Club first. We would book a room, although we hoped not to use it, but this was a sort of place for the GIs in town. They had a bulletin board where you could check to see if any of your buddies were in town and John and I always put our name up. We didn't have any buddies off base that we wanted to find, we did it just so that it looked like we belonged. I do remember meeting a lady of the night around the circus, a sweet young thing; she came from Scotland. The night we met we had just got back to her room when the alarm sounded. She was terrified and shaking with fear. I remember we got under her bed and I put my arms around her and held her tight all night. For some strange reason I felt really good in the morning – sweet thing, I will always remember her. Down where the docks were was our favourite haunt, down where all the bombing had been' [probably the East End]. 'You saw more of life here, more of the real England and the English. They were such nice people; they welcomed us and made us part of their life. Being in this part we weren't bothered by MPs and the SPs so much, they all stayed around the bright lights area. The girls were great and we would be sure of a good night out with them. They took us to some unusual pubs to say the least and I am sure many of the guys there were on the wrong side of the law, but that didn't worry us. As the saying goes, we could be dead tomorrow. They would also take us to what they called "Drinking Houses", I am not sure what the difference was except they did not look like real pubs. We taught them the game of "craps"; they found the name amusing. We did tend to forget the difference in money and we often treated your pounds the same as our dollar, forgetting there was a difference of about three to one. They didn't mind, pound notes were floating about like ticker tape. The British Bobbies seemed to be different there too, they were always friendly and would stop and chat to us, never hassled us at all. They seemed to know most of the girls by name as well.

'It did seem strange to see all the area flattened. Sometimes it was whole streets that had gone, but the people just carried on as though nothing had happened. They were just great. I remember one amusing thing that happened one night. My buddy John and I were in an area where everything had been flattened except a pub which stood all on its own amongst the rubble. We decided we would go in for a drink and I remember the place was very dark and only lit by kerosene lamps. After a while John said he was going out the back to relieve himself. He had been gone sometime and I began to worry what had happened to him so I thought I'd better go and look for him. When I went into the toilets, the urinal was empty but I could hear moaning coming from one of the cubicles. I pushed open the door only to find there was no floor but the moaning was definitely coming from there. I shone my torch down to see John lying on his back on rubble about twelve feet down, still with his pants undone and moaning. I rushed back into the bar and told the bar tender what had happened and he sent somebody for the NFS. A little guy arrived with a ladder and went down and hoisted John on his back and carried him up as though he was a rag doll. John stood well over six feet and it always amazed me how this little guy just threw John over his shoulder like he was nothing. Fortunately John did not really hurt himself, apart from a few bruises and the most difficult part was trying to clean up his uniform as he had a stream of wet mud down his pants. We enjoyed our London trips, but we did seem to get through a hell of a lot of money when we were there. I don't think we ever slept much as there was always too much to do and only a couple of days to do it in. When we did sleep, I remember waking up once or twice in some strange places and often as not with some very strange woman. The only drawback to our trips was that we had to attend the infirmary for two or three days afterwards to get rid of anything we might have caught. Fortunately neither John nor I seemed to have caught anything we shouldn't have.'

CHAPTER TEN

The 'Witch'

The 467th did not have any heroes as we would know them, but they did have a hero plane, known as *Witchcraft*, or the *Witch*. But little did the men who built the *Witch* realise she was to become the most talked about and the most revered plane in the entire Eighth Air Force and would be known throughout the United States, not only for her exploits, but for her ground crew as well.

The *Witch* was built by Boeing at their San Diego Consolidated plant. She was given a number just like all other aircraft at the time. Aircraft number H15-42-52534 was allocated to the 467th and was destined to fly to Rackheath.

The crew which first took command of H15-42-52534 was led by Lt George Reed. They were due to start their 'tour' of operations from Rackheath, having done the required training in the desert. Most of the crew were boys aged around nineteen or twenty years old. Lt Reed, however, was given the nickname of 'Pappy' Reed and to these boys he was a very old man of just twenty-six years.

'Pappy' Reed and his crew flew to Rackheath via the 'southern ferry route' along with the rest of the aircraft bound for Rackheath. It was while on this flight that the crew decided their aircraft needed a name and after much discussion settled on the name *Witchcraft*. It was while they were in a stop-over at Belem, Brazil, that the flight engineer, Robert De Kerf, was elected to paint the 'nose art' on the plane. The symbol was to be of a witch sitting astride a gun and holding a bomb in one hand.

On one occasion whilst the *Witch* was flying over water, the crew had just eaten lunch that was supplied to them in small boxes, measuring some eight inches square by four inches deep. On completion of lunch one of the crew said he wanted to go to the loo (it was not the kind of job where he could use the relief tube, it was a bigger job than that). He was told he would have to wait until he landed at their next stop-over. He complained strongly that he could not wait and informed the pilot he would use one of the empty lunch boxes, seal the lid and drop it out the front nose wheel escape hatch into the sea. Job done, he opened the escape hatch to drop the box out. Unfortunately, when the escape hatch was opened, it caused an 'up' draft with the effect that the box began dancing around the nose of the plane. The inevitable happened and the lid came off, scattering the contents into the whirling air. The contents stuck to everything, including the pilot and co-pilot's boots, the rudder pedals and the guns in nose canopy. It took ages to clean up the aircraft and get some fresh air into it. Needless to say this stunt was never tried again.

Joe Ramirez and *Witchcraft*

The aircraft arrived at Rackheath and was assigned to the 790th Sqn. The ground crew assigned to her became almost as famous as the plane. The ground chief was Private First Class Joe Ramirez, a man of Mexican descent. He found it strange that the rest of the crew were of higher rank than he, and yet he had to give them orders. The rest of the crew were made up of George Dong, of Chinese descent, Joe Vetter, of Dutch descent, Ray Betcher, of German descent and Walter Elliot, American. So started a first class partnership that was to become known as 'The League of Nations' crew. They formed such a strong bond together that they are still friends and keep in touch with each other. When Joe was asked why he was put in charge of men senior in rank to himself, he thought maybe it was because he had worked in auto shops and had majored in mechanics in junior and high school.

This crew grew to love the *Witch*. Even a simple oil leak was a major disaster and she was cleaned and serviced every time she came home from a mission. Joe and his crew worked tirelessly to keep this aircraft in tip-top order. They would often work through the night if the *Witch* came back from a mission with some fault or damage – nothing was too much trouble for their beloved plane. The *Witch* flew 130 missions without failing to reach the target; not all in one piece but she never missed a mission. This was a record.

She was however almost lost before she had completed thirty missions. According to Flight Engineer Robert De Kerf: 'We had made our run over the target, dropped our bombs and were heading for home. It was my job to check that all bombs had gone and none were hung up in the bomb bay. On this occasion I found not one bomb, but two. One was stuck in the bomb bay doors stopping them from closing up properly and because of this, the bomb bay doors were jammed. They could neither be opened to let the bomb out, or be closed. At the same time, a second bomb was rolling about in the bomb bay with both its nose and tail propellers spinning, thus arming the bomb. I did the only thing I could do. I jumped down into the bomb bay and picked up the 100 lb bomb at each end to stop the propellers spinning. I had no idea how long they had been going or if the bomb was about to go off. Whilst holding the bomb, I kicked at the bomb bay doors to try to open them. Eventually I succeeded and the bomb fell out. I quickly dropped the other bomb out through the bomb bay doors and hoped it would not explode directly beneath the aircraft. Fortunately both bombs dropped clear. I gave a great sigh of relief, I can tell you.'

During her fortuitous career the *Witch* flew 65 missions to Germany, 31 to France and 4 to Belgium. She sustained over 300 flak holes, had 15

Changing *Witchcraft*'s engine

engine changes, due to either flak damage, engines being totally shot away or just simply worn out, and dropped over 500,000 lbs of bombs.

On one occasion, when the *Witch* flew on a mission to Neunkirchen, Germany, she was badly shot up and lost one engine. The other engines were overheating and the crew did not think she was going to get home. However, they did manage to coax her over the English coast but she was in such a bad state that they were forced to land at the first air base they could find. It happened to be Manston on the south coast. They landed on a very muddy airstrip and looked at the sorry state of their aircraft and considered themselves lucky. This was 28th December 1944. Manston telephoned Rackheath and told them that the *Witch* was 'US' so badly was she beaten up.

On hearing about this, Joe Ramirez persuaded Col Shower to allow him to take his crew to Manston and see if they could save the *Witch*. Col Shower agreed to let him try as good aircraft were not easy to come by. Joe, his chief assistant George Dong, and Ray Betcher set off with a lorry containing a spare engine, tools and various bits and pieces. They worked non-stop on a cold wet airstrip. The *Witch* had so many broken 'bones' it should have been the end of her, but they brought her back to life. They would not let her die and within a few days she was back at Rackheath, battered but alive and well.

There were to be three other occasions when the *Witch* was to lose engines over the target or on missions, but because there was very little other damage, she was able to make it back home. One of these missions took place on 7th January 1945. It does get a bit confusing here because this was her 98th mission. It should have been her 100th mission but she had previously set out on two other missions and had been recalled before reaching the target. Those two did not count.

The *Witch* was being piloted by Lt G. G. (Casy) Lazlo. They had just got out over the North Sea, when an engine misfired and died. Casy, having been told that this was the 100th mission for the *Witch*, was in a dilemma. Should he turn back as he was supposed to do and face the wrath of Col Shower and the whole of the base, or should he go on and hope to make the return journey? After much mental anguish, he thought anything was better than facing the problems he would have if he turned back. He decided to go on. Fortunately for him the mission was generally without mishap, and he returned safely, much to the delight of Col Shower and the entire base. No other aircraft had ever reached its 100th mission and a big party ensued.

As a result of the 100 up, Joe Ramirez and his crew were congratulated by Major General William F. Kepner, second Bombardment Division Commander; Brigadier General Walter R. Peck, 96th Combat Wing Commander and Major Fred Holdrege, 790th Bombardment squadron Commander, for 'their meritorious achievement in the performance of their outstanding services'. Joe Ramirez received an Oak Leaf Cluster to add to his Bronze Star. The other four received 'Certificates of Meritorious Service', signed by Brigadier General Peck himself. The true 100th for *Witch* took place some six days later, on 13th January 1945. On this occasion she was flown by Lt J. W. Rice jnr.

It was said that some pilots complained that when the *Witch* was in flight one wing would always be lower than the other, thus making the pilot have to keep correcting the trim. The story goes that Joe and his crew spent hours and hours trying to correct this problem, but to no avail. Finally the problem was solved by removing the offending wing tip and inserting 20 lbs of lead ballast. Joe has made no comment on this story, but other ground chiefs have been consulted and most are of the opinion that this is a fairy story.

In the end the *Witch* flew some 130 missions, clocking up 665 mission flying hours. She had been battered and beaten beyond belief, but still she flew. Any aircraft flying over Rackheath, could pick out the *Witch* from all the rest. When most of the remaining planes were of the newer unpainted variety, she was still in her original olive drab camouflage that had been patched up so many times with different coloured material that she looked more like Joseph's coat of many colours than the grand old lady that she was. Without exception, all the air crews who flew her (and there were many) said that they knew they would get home; the old lady would look after them. I think her greatest achievement was, that of all the crews which flew in her, not one was ever killed or injured. She did indeed look after them all.

In June 1945 *Witchcraft* said goodbye to Rackheath. She was to be flown back to the States. She had taken part in the first mission flown by the 467th and everyone up to the last but one. The now famous ground crew said goodbye to her and returned to their civilian lives. The *Witch* was almost the last aircraft to leave Rackheath. She returned to the States a heroine. She went on a tour of America to promote the sale of war bonds but sadly the time came when she, like a lot of wartime aircraft, was scrapped. It is reported that she was sold for next to nothing. The buyers made more money out of the petrol they siphoned out of her tanks, than they paid for the whole aircraft. It is such a shame that the government did not have the foresight to preserve this aircraft for posterity.

This was not to be the end of the name *Witchcraft*. After hostilities had ceased, the American Air Force had a display under the Eiffel Tower in Paris of all the types of aircraft used during the war. Amongst the aircraft displayed was a B-24 Liberator with the nose 'art' of a Witch sitting on a gun carrying a bomb. Its colours were that of the 790th squadron of the 467th. Its name – *Witchcraft II*!

This following story, which occurred before 'Witchcraft' was named, was told to me by Col Fred Holdrege (then Captain) who was on a training flight. It is known as 'The Tale of the Jackalope'.

According to the log of Lt John Oder, co-pilot aboard 52534, the 790th Squadron of the 467th, took off from Casper Army Air Base on February 5th 1944. It was to be the last mission from that base before returning to Wendover Field to complete its training in preparation for overseas movement.

It was a bright sunny day with perfect vision, when '52534' joined an assembly of a six aircraft formation over the base prior to its departure for Thermopolis, a city some one hundred and twenty miles to the north west. The formation was led by Lt Robert Sheehan with Capt. Fred Holdrege as Command pilot in the co-pilot seat. Lt Sheehan led the Squadron over the Wind River Canyon en route to its primary target.

Over the city of Thermopolis, Captain Holdrege saw the opportunity to provide a realistic practise bomb run that was similar to the raid on Ploesti oil fields which had taken place earlier in the hostilities (this raid was to make the B-24 famous – flying just a few feet off the ground). After the initial run over the city, a circle was made to allow the approach to come in from the west. The formation turned and descended to zero feet for the bomb run. This was to bring them over Capt. Holdrege's grandfather's ranch, the Ember Ranch. Being so low, the tremendous noise caused a herd of Jackalopes to scatter. A ranch hand was trying to brand a steer at the time, he got so enraged, that he threw the branding iron at the incoming aircraft, striking aircraft 52534 on the tail. Thus the aircraft later to be named *Witchcraft* got the letter 'M' printed upon its tail.

After making a successful bombing run the formation turned to the right and immediately commenced its 500 ft per minute climb, to clear the Wind River Mountains to the south and passing just over Three Mile Bridge. The return to Casper Army Air Base was uneventful. The mission lasted four hours, thirty minutes, according to Lt John Oders' log. The way this practise mission was carried out, was to hold them in good stead later during their tour of duty over Europe. They were to destroy a very important bridge over the Seine. The low level accurate bombing run was remembered from the Thermopolis practise mission.

'Witch' way

LT HENSLEY FLIES DAMAGED PLANE HOME

Lt Baxter Hensley of Springdale is a hero to his crew on the Liberator Bomber *Also Ran*. In action over Europe, when badly damaged with shell he was able to bring his ship home safe. The story was released to 'The News'.

AN EIGHTH AIRFORCE LIBERATOR BOMBER STATION, ENGLAND.

The Liberator Bomber *Also Ran*, 20,000 feet over her target and with bomb bay doors open, received a near fatal blow when three bursting flak shells, the third almost in her bomb bay, sent her reeling. With severed gasoline and hydraulic lines and her number one and number three motors knocked out, the Bomber's plight was desperate. Balanced precariously on the catwalk, with a 20,000 foot void yawning below him, T/Sgt Henry W Ellison of 1123 Seventh ST. Rosenberg, Texas, strove to repair the damage. He was drenched with highly inflammable fuel and the catwalk was slippery in the extreme, affording scant foothold. As he stretched toward the side of the ship, to stop the spurting gas, he was steadied by T/Sgt Raymond Tiron of Campbell, Minnesota who also held his oxygen bottle. Temporarily plugging the break in the gas line with one hand, T/Sgt Ellison located and shut off the valve controlling the flow. The hydraulic line was then 'pinched off' and the escape of that fluid halted.

The big Liberator was losing altitude rapidly and the chances of reaching England seemed to be slim indeed. Her bombs were released and guns, ammunition, flak suits, camera and tools were jettisoned in an attempt to lighten her load. With consummate skill the pilot, 2nd Lt Baxter W Hensley of Springdale, Arkansas nursed the wounded ship towards her home base and managed to retain sufficient altitude to bring his plane over a nearby fighter field. [This was RAF Coltishall, a fighter base with grass runways.] After making a perfect landing the crew were amazed to learn that this had been accomplished despite the fact that one of the ship's tires had been flat, punctured by flak. The entire crew are loud in their praises of Lt Hensley's skill and he in turn is very proud of his 'team'.

From an unknown American newspaper

THE TALE OF THE JACKALOPE

A Jackalope was a mythical animal the Westerners of the United States invented for the gullible Easterners. The Easterners were told always to look out for 'Herds of Jackalopes' when coming out west, as they were dangerous. In fact a Jackalope was nothing more than a stuffed Jack Rabbit with antlers glued on to its head.

The story as told did take place with the exception of the Jackalopes and the branding iron leaving an imprint on the tail of 'Witchcraft'. The letter 'M' that appears on the plane is a squadron marking. This part of the story was told as a practical joke by Col Holdrege.

CHAPTER ELEVEN

Farewell

Mid April 1945 was to see the last big party the 467th were to have at Rackheath. The group had completed its 200th mission. They had flown into hostile territory nearly every day since arriving, and many could see it was all nearly over. Unfortunately, there was to be a sad end to this party.

As part of the celebrations Col Shower had arranged a flying display by some P-51 Mustangs. The Mustangs had played a big part in escorting and defending the Liberators on their missions. Part of the display was to be the Mustangs flying inverted under the aerial antenna that ran from the control tower to a pole some hundred yards away. This aerial was only fifty feet off the ground. Unfortunately, while this was taking place, another Mustang not connected with the display strayed into the area. On seeing the other Mustangs going under the wire, he thought they were beating up the field just for devilment, and decided to have a go under the wire himself. Sadly he did not make it, his wing tip caught the ground and he ploughed straight into the ground. He did not survive the crash. No one felt like celebrating after that.

So ended the occupation of the 467th Heavy Bombardment Group at Rackheath. Their last mission was their two hundred and twelfth, and took place on 25th April 1945. On 6th June the first aircraft left the base to return home and they were leaving virtually every day from then on. The last one departed on 6th July 1945. In the intervening time, several of the aircraft took sightseeing trips over France and Germany. They took five or six of the ground staff at a time, thus enabling the ground crew to see the devastation caused when they had sent their charges out on a mission.

The 467th were in England for just fourteen months. In that period, they flew 212 combat missions, 5,538 combat sorties with an average of 26 aircraft per mission and dropped a total 13,353 tons of bombs, or 2.4 tons per aircraft per sortie. Aircraft lost in action numbered only 29, the lowest loss rate of any group in the Eight Air Force, but 242 men were killed in action

Souvenir banknote issued for the 200th Mission Party

or killed in the line of duty. For many their final resting place was to be the American War Cemetery at Madingley, Cambridge. Some aircraft were flown back to the States, others were never recovered and 20 were lost in accidents. Enemy aircraft claims were 6 destroyed, 5 probable and 2 damaged. The Group set an unsurpassed record of bombing accuracy for the entire Eighth Air Force. Even the Photo Section received citations for the photos secured. The Group had its fair share of decorations and promotions. The 467th was one of the best units in the entire Eighth Air Force, holding most of the records for achievement and dedication to duty, including in some cases putting one hundred per cent of its bombs on the target. The Commanding General of the 96th Combat Wing wrote the following to Col Albert J Shower:

'The records clearly indicate the continuous outstanding performance of the 467th Group in all phases of operation. Most commendable is the absence of any slumps in your bombing records. You have been at or near the top throughout. It is proof of the initiative, tenacity of purpose, and drive exercised by you and your command.'

This must surely prove that all four Squadron Commanders, Junior Officers and men had the greatest trust and admiration for their Group Commander, Colonel Albert Joseph Shower and prove that the iron rod wielded by 'Black Al' surely paid off.

Most of the local population were sorry to see the '467' go. The Americans had after all brought a whole new world to this once quiet corner of Norfolk and life would not be the same again. Many of the locals had enjoyed the company of these young men with a strange way of speaking. Many had enjoyed their first taste of things like chewing gum and chocolate bars and many local girls had worn nylon stockings for the first time in their lives. Some had been guests on the base and had danced to the strains of the 'Airliners', the band the Americans had formed from base personnel. Some had even learned a new-fangled dance called the 'Jitterbug'. In many cases, the first thing the locals remember is 'the damned noise from them damned planes all day and night' and it's only when they are pressed that a few of them smile and speak fondly of the American invasion. Without exception they all speak of the generosity of the Americans, not just flashing their money around, but genuinely caring for the people in and around the area. It comes across how much they looked after the children when they threw a Christmas party in the village hall. It was the first time many of the children had tasted ice cream and the Americans often gave the children sweets and goodies to take home for their families. When the Americans visited the local pubs the children would gather at the entrance and offer to 'look after' the cycles while the men were inside. For this they would receive two shillings or even half a crown (10p or 12½p – a formidable amount in those days), but the children never took their job seriously. As the men came out of the pub, usually the worse for wear, the children would give them the first bike they got hold of and off the servicemen would go, wobbling down the road. Very few of them got back the cycle they came with. Ted Jeremy, a lively twelve year old, remembers this well. He would look after the bikes at the Bell in Salhouse and he remembers one night when it was very foggy and the men could not find their way back to base. Ted ran to get his father who showed the men a short cut through the back lanes to the base. A few days later when Ted's father was working on his allotment, some Americans cycled past and threw a pair of strong leather boots and a big piece of ham over the fence and shouted 'thanks for getting us home buddy'. Ted remembers his father wore those boots for years after the war.

Many remember the Americans visiting their houses on Sundays. There was a leaflet printed for the Americans to tell them how to behave in England and one of the items said that they should not eat too much when invited to an English home as what would be put on the table would almost certainly be a week's ration for the household. For this reason many of the Americans, when invited to the house, would bring tins of Libby's peaches, cheese and various other goodies. Word of this soon got around and suddenly the Americans were inundated with invites to visit folk in their homes.

Some were genuine invites. Joy Wilde remembers several of the Americans visiting her house. Her mum and dad would make them feel welcome and some would just come and sit around the fire and talk about home. It was clear they were very homesick. Joy remembers her mother doing the washing for the lads and sometimes she would do someone's washing and it would not be collected. They had been on a mission and never returned and Joy remembers her mother often having a cry when the boys did not come back. She had grown attached to some of them; they even called her 'mom'.

Peter Smith tells an amusing story of 'pubbing missions'. He was a seventeen year old and rode a motorcycle and because of the blackout he had only slits for lights on his bike so he could not see very far in front. One night he was coming home after dark just at 'chucking out' time at the King's Head at Blofield. He came round the corner and ran straight into a group of Americans just about to mount their trusty steeds to go home. He did not hurt any of them but he did buckle the front wheel of one of the cycles and with a group of Americans the worse for wear, he thought he was in for a good hiding. To his surprise they laughed it off and asked him

THE 467TH BOMBARDMENT GROUP (H) STATION 145

U.S. ARMY AIR FORCES

200TH MISSION PARTY

SATURDAY, 21 APRIL :: SUNDAY, 22 APRIL, 1945

★

A GREETING from the Commanding Officer to every member of the 467th Group and all Allied Units

Each and every member of the 467th Group and Allied Units may well view with pride and satisfaction the enviable record established in carrying out in less than a year, two hundred bombing attacks against enemy installations, as well as numerous efficiently run "trucking" missions—hauling supplies to rapidly moving ground forces during September 1944. The record has been outstanding because of the unfailing interest, untiring devotion to duty and wholehearted co-operation of all officers and men on this station, both on the ground and in the air. Your co-ordinated efforts have resulted in relentless attrition upon the enemy's resources and fighting facilities, and you may feel rightfully conscious that yours was a tangible contribution toward the impending final triumph of Allied Arms.

While giving thanks for past success, let us be mindful of the sacrifice made by those who have not returned from these missions. Their only request would undoubtedly be that we continue during the ensuing months of the war to display that same zeal and enthusiasm which have during the past year achieved such splendid results, to the end that we may see chastisement of the last aggressors and the establishment of a just and lasting peace.

ALBERT J. SHOWER, Colonel, Air Corps Commanding.

An Invitation

PROGRAM
OVERLEAF

The 200th Mission cake

Going home

if he knew where they could store the bike for the night. Peter's parents owned the Post Office at the time, so he offered to keep it there and with that the Americans said they would be back the next night to collect it and off they went riding two up on the bikes. Sure enough the following night they were back. Peter was astounded to see that they had welded two lugs on the back forks of one of the bikes and had wing nuts threaded on the lugs. They took up the broken bike, dropped the front wheel and hitched the front forks on to the lugs, did up the wing nuts, hopped on and away they went. Peter said it was the funniest sight you ever did see because of course the two were peddling at different times in a sort of articulated tandem.

Joan Chapman (nee Curtis) as a sixteen year old remembers that when the young air crew came back, they would walk away from the planes like zombies. 'They looked like real old men, nothing like the same boys we would see during their visits to the pubs or coming into the village. Joan's mother, who was Aggie Curtis, would help with the catering when the Americans held the monthly dances. She too always talks about their kindness and she remembers that, when her sister had a birthday, the cook from the base made her a sumptuous cake, something that would have been out of the question in wartime for the civilian population. She remembers too, watching the planes go out early in the morning and being anxious until their return. 'Mother and I would count them back in and it was always sad when one or two did not come back or we would see some of them come back with big holes in them or with their engines smoking. You could not help but feel very sorry for those young boys.'

One or two of the local ladies found a sideline to improve their standard of living and found themselves very popular with the Americans. Molly and Mary (their names have been changed) were two such ladies. They found the Americans to be a strange bunch but they talk fondly of how the boys always treated them like ladies and not as something to be used and then put down. Molly remembers that some officers just wanted company and to talk, nothing more, and they paid well for the privilege, whereas others wanted a good time. She remembers they all took the attitude that they were not going to make it through the war.

There was a club for the Americans in the village of Wroxham some two miles from the base. This club was for all intents and purposes a social club but it seems in most cases it was just a front for entertaining the ladies. Apparently it was formed for the sole purpose of taking the ladies off the street out of sight of the public so as not to offend public decency. Both Molly and Mary were regular visitors to this club which was used mainly by officers. Apparently some wild parties went on within its confines. Of the 'other ranks' Molly and Mary say they very rarely used the club, their domain was the bomb blast shelter situated just off Green Lane (still clearly visible today). If the ladies' services were required by the other ranks, they were always taken to this shelter. Mary remembers that when you went in it was dark, but the men were lined up shoulder to shoulder with other girls and you had to fight for a space. Everything was done standing up. Both Molly and Mary knew nearly all the girls and said that one or two were married with husbands overseas. Some of the girls came in from Norwich, but it's not clear how they got there or indeed how they got back as the bus service was very sparse in those days. One crew member does confirm that there were several local ladies willing to 'share' their favours with the men and he knew one or two were under age. For his part he felt it too risky with the local girls. 'The women in London or from Norwich were OK but with the local girls, nah it was far too dodgy, I kept well out of that.' But suffice it to say, it seems the needs of the Americans were well taken care of in one form or another. As for Molly and Mary, when the Americans left they did not continue to ply their trade. They returned to their normal lives and both eventually married and raised families. Some would not voice their memories of the American invasion; they would just smile and say nothing but a definite twinkle could be seen in their eye.

The base was returned to the RAF and on 4th August 1945 it was deactivated. The RAF kept the 231st Maintenance Sub Unit at the base for a while; this consisted of some thirty men and a cookhouse. The hangars were used to store unwanted bombs and flares, and other bits and pieces of surplus equipment were stored in and around the airfield.

In 1959 the RAF left the base for good and the summer of 1960 saw a crop spraying company take over. They stayed for two or three years, and about this time the first of the industrial units moved in.

Sadly only a small number of the buildings still remain; one hangar has been revamped to look a bit more modern. A small section of the main runway is still visible, half way up Muck Lane, which runs parallel to Green Lane. If you look really hard you can see one or two of the hard stands where a plane would stand at dispersal. Part of the old control tower is still there, but the radio shack is missing and the entire building is in a general state of disrepair.

On the other side of Green Lane several of the living quarters still stand, very much overgrown and in a bad state of repair. The gymnasium, blast trenches and several of the offices are still there, but unfortunately, these are on private property and not generally open to the public. Some of the drawings and pictures painted by the men of the 467th are still visible on

Rackheath Air Base today

the walls of some of the billets. There is a memorial stone situated on the industrial estate and the Rackheath village sign does include a Liberator as part of its badge. This is near the Sole and Heel pub.

As the generations go by the memories and physical signs of this once busy base fade away. The landscape has changed and will go on changing until such time as the only thing remaining will be the memorial stone in a small corner. Those who survived went back to loved ones and tried to return to normal life. They came as young boys, they returned home old men, old not in years but in their minds. They had suffered from watching their friends die, in some cases right in front of their eyes, and from just trying to survive. Many recall how it took several years for them to adapt to normal living. Others, were cut down in their youth and never got to experience their own family lives. They may be buried in some distant land far from their loved ones, but they should not be forgotten.

The people of Rackheath and the people of Great Britain can only say thank you to the boys of the 467th and the entire Eighth Air Force for their part in helping to win the war.

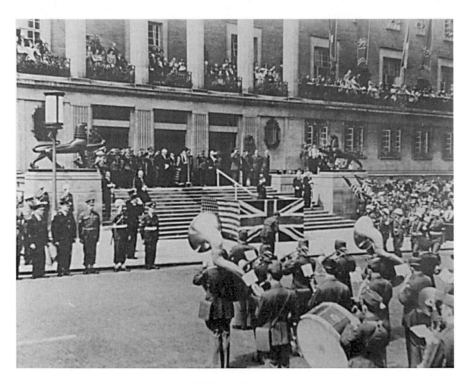

VE Day, Norwich

Shoulder flashes

AUTHOR'S NOTE

As a footnote to this story, I have read other bits and pieces about the 467th, and some tell it slightly differently to my version. I believe my account to be accurate. I have not 'pinched' bits out of other books and I have tried to cross check all my information before writing it down. I have however quoted one or two articles from other books, but these have been clearly stated at the beginning of the article and only then when I have been able to substantiate them. As the reader can see, this is not a history of the 467th; it is a story, a true story, but never the less, a story. I hope you will now go on and chase up the full facts about these young men and their exploits. I must make a confession here. I have lived very close to this base for some twelve or more years but I did not know it existed. I discovered the fact by accident and had a mild interest in it as it was right on my doorstep. When I asked a few questions I became so fascinated that I had to go on. I hope I have given you a small insight into this subject and that it grips you like it gripped me and that you will want to go on. There are many more stories connected to the 467th. I have told of just a few of them, and now it's up to you to seek more of the fascinating information to be had.

I have included some technical data in the back of this book, showing the relevant sites. I have also included one or two funny bits of paper that some 'wag' posted around the base.

B24 Liberator takeoff crew positions

No crew rear of waist window

No crew in bomb bay

No crew in nose compartment
(in case of front wheel collapse)

B24 Liberator operational crew positions

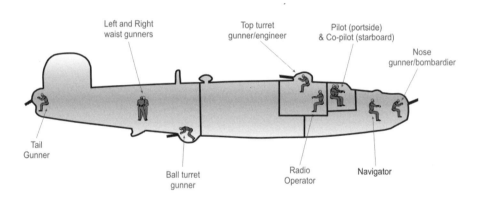

Left and Right waist gunners

Top turret gunner/engineer

Pilot (portside) & Co-pilot (starboard)

Nose gunner/bombardier

Tail Gunner

Ball turret gunner

Radio Operator

Navigator

B-24 crew positions (© *Kenton White*)

96TH COMBAT WING
467TH BOMBARDMENT GROUP (HEAVY)
(The Rackheath Aggies)
Station 145
Call Sign, Decktray

First mission flown, 10th April 1944. Last mission 25th April 1945

788th Bombardment Squadron (Heavy)   Code X7 (No plus or bar sign)

789th Bombardment Squadron (Heavy)   Code 6A (Bar above Aircraft Letter)

790th Bombardment Squadron (Heavy)   Code Q2 (Bar below Aircraft Letter)

791st Bombardment Squadron (Heavy)   Code 4Z (Plus sign after Letter)

NUMBER OF MISSIONS IN THE ETO
221 are recorded but 9 of these missions were recalled prior to the aircraft reaching the target. They therefore did not count towards the tally. Only 212 were in fact flown to and bombed the target.

LENGTH OF STAY AT RACKHEATH
Official arrival 12th March 1944.   Official departure 5th July 1945.

OPERATIONAL LOSSES
29 Aircraft Missing in Action. 19 other Operational losses. Total 48 Aircraft.

AUTHENTICATED ENEMY FIGHTERS LOST TO THE 467TH BG
4 Me 109s destroyed. 1 Me 109 Probable. 2 FW 109s destroyed. 1 FW 190 Probable and 2 FW 190s damaged.

[99]

ALLIIERTES ...KOMMANDO
(Supreme Headquart... ...Expeditionary Force)

AN DIE DEUTSCHEN
EISENBAHNER

·Deutsche Eisenbahner !

Ihr erkennt bereits, dass die Wucht der alliierten Luftoffensive dauernd zunimmt. Es war unausbleiblich, dass Ihr dabei schwere Verluste an Toten und Verwundeten zu beklagen habt.

Eure Eisenbahnen dienen nur drei Zwecken :

ERSTENS führen sie der Front Nachschub und Verstärkungen zu. Dieser Nachschub und diese Verstärkungen können nur dazu dienen, den verlorenen Krieg zu verlängern und dadurch die Verwüstung Eurer Heime und die Zahl der toten und verwundeten Soldaten und Zivilpersonen noch zu vergrössern.

ZWEITENS werden Eure Eisenbahnen dazu benützt, um den invasionsbedrohten Gebieten die Lebensmittel, Vorräte und sonstigen Einrichtungen zu entziehen, welche diese Gebiete noch diesen Winter dringend benötigen werden.

DRITTENS werden sie dazu verwendet, Hundert-·

German leaflet

[100]

TO THE GERMAN

RAILWAY WORKERS

German Railway Workers

You will have realised by now that the might of the Allied Air Offensive increases all the time. It was inevitable that you would suffer many deaths and injuries.

Your railways serve only three purposes:

FIRSTLY they take supplies and reinforcements to the front. These supplies and reinforcements can only serve to lengthen the already lost war and to bring more destruction of your homeland and increase the numbers of dead and wounded soldiers and civilians.

SECONDLY your trains are being used to withdraw food, supplies and other equipment from those areas threatened by invasion though the people in these areas will have urgent need of these supplies this winter.

THIRDLY they are used . . .

German leaflet translation

STANDING ORDERS
Issued to every man on the base, regardless of rank or position.

Headquarters
Office of the Commanding Officer
Station 145   APO 634
15 March 1944
Station instructions

General Information	Mess Hours	
This is Station AAF # 145	Officers	Enlisted Men
Telephone (official) Norwich 25191	0700–0815	0630–0745
A.P.O. 634	1130–1300	1130–1300
	1730–1900	1700–1830

UNIFORM
All personnel, both Commissioned and Enlisted men, leaving this station on official business, pass, furlough or leave, will wear class 'A' Uniform. Blouses will be worn by Officers at the evening meal. Neckties will be worn by Officers while on duty. Fatigue uniform may be worn by Enlisted men off the Station on work detail.

FURLOUGHS, LEAVES AND PASSES
Furloughs and leaves cannot be granted until after three (3) months have elapsed since arrival over-seas.
Consult the Adjutant for pass regulations.

MAIL
All mail sent by US Army personnel must be mailed in an ARMY POST OFFICE. Mail or Telegrams from within the UK to US Army personnel must be addressed as follows
    (Rank) John Q. Doe
    unit attached to
    APO #634
    US Army
Mail for British addresses must bear British postage. Postal Money Orders can be purchased from the Army Post Office. Facilities for wiring home may be arranged through personnel.

AEROCLUB
The Red Cross Aeroclub is open from 1100 hours to 2300 hours. The snack bar is open from 1800 hours to 2200 hours.

FIELD DIRECTOR
The Red Cross Field Director, Mr Ralph E. Adams, has his office in the Aeroclub and is anxious to serve all men who have problems of any kind. Both Aeroclub and Field Directors office are set up to help and serve you in every way possible.

OFFICERS REPORTING FOR DUTY
All Officers reporting for duty at this Station will register in the Adjutant's Office. They will also report themselves to the Officers Mess Officer to arrange Messing facilities
Officers, when leaving this Station during Duty hours, or on leave in excess of six (6) hours, will sign out in the Adjutant's Office.

TRAFFIC
All traffic in England keeps to the LEFT of the road. Pedestrian traffic will walk facing the traffic. No one will walk on any but the paved roads while on this Base, giving strictest attention to Camouflage Discipline. Do not walk more than two abreast. Walk in single file at night. In crossing streets, be careful to look RIGHT before stepping off the curb.

BLACKOUT
Blackout Regulations must be strictly observed. It means the security of your Station and the lives of the Troops. Blackout hour will be designated by loudspeaker (Tannoy) announcement.

BICYCLES
During the hours of Blackout, bicycles will be ridden with both head and tail lights. Two or more persons riding a bicycle is prohibited. Bicycles will not be borrowed. The purchase of, or the possession of a bicycle without a proper bill of sale or Military Authority is in direct violation of both civil and Military law. Military Personnel, before purchasing a bicycle, new or used, will first clarify the proposed transaction with the Provost Marshal. Violation of these instructions will be severely dealt with.

MOVIES
Movies are shown approximately four (4) times per week in the Sgt's Mess – Mess Site.

GAS MASKS
Wednesday of each week, all Personnel, Officers and enlisted men will carry their gas masks during the hours of 0800 and 1600.

RATION OF FUEL

Coal and coke must be strictly rationed in the ETO. This Station is allowed 56 lbs of coal or coke per man per week. From this is deducted coal used in mess halls, administrative buildings, tech site etc, which leaves only 112 lbs per week for each stove located in billets.

QUARTERS

1. Leave your hut in a neat, clean condition when you leave the Station. It might be occupied again on short notice.
2. Personnel, both Commissioned and Enlisted men are prohibited from changing quarters without the authority of the Billiting Officer.

CONDUCT OF TROOPS

Each unit Commander will demand of his troops, good behaviour and manners, on or off this Station. A smart soldierly bearing and strict attention to saluting at all times.

TRANSPORTATION FACILITIES

Convoys for Liberty run will leave PX area each evening at 1830 hours from Norwich, returning at 2300 hours.

The convoy Commander will inspect the troops for uniforms and proper appearance prior to departure from this Station. He is responsible for the discipline enroute and the observance of speed regulations. No stops are allowed. Drivers will remain with their vehicles during the entire Liberty run.

Commercial Bus Service is available on the Wroxham Road, at both entrances, running approximately every 45 minutes during the day.

Taxis are permitted to enter the Base only to site 5 and the Officers Club.

Bus numbers 5, 5a, & 9 leave Surry Street Station to this Base. Last Bus from town is #91 from Thorpe Station to the Blue Boar at 8:55 pm.

Commanding officers (from left): Lt Col Herzberg, Doenges, Col Albert Shower, Lt Col Walter R. Smith, Maj Ned Ogden

ATTENTION

What to do in case of an Air Raid

1. In case of an Air Raid, run like hell, it does not matter where you are, just so long as you run. If you are outside, run inside. If you are inside, run outside. It is also suggested that you equip yourself with track shoes, so you have no trouble getting over people in front of you.

2. Always make the most of an Air Raid.

    A. If you are in a Bakery, steal a Pie.

    B. If you are in a Bar, grab a bottle.

    C. If you are in the Movies, grab a Blonde.

3. During an Air Raid, yell bloody murder, it makes more confusion.

4. If you find an unexploded Bomb, shake it, the firing pin may be stuck.

5. If an Incendiary Bomb falls in your neighbourhood, throw Gasolene on it.

6. Always eat Garlic and wear dirty socks before entering an Air Raid Shelter, it will make you as popular as a Skunk in the Opera, but it will releive the crowded shelter conditions.

7. Dont pay any attention to the Air Raid Warden, if he gets in your way, run over him, all he knows is more confusion. One of them may know what is best for you, but that is what Folk used to know when they fed you Castor Oil.

8. Dont worry about a bomb that has your name on it, its the one labled 'To whom it may concern' that you ought to worry about.

9. Keep calm during an Air Raid, try this formular, read the Lords Prayer. Bless 'Ike and Mc Arthur, take a slug of whiskey, say another prayer and repeat this process. Dont forget the Prayers until all the whiskey is gone, then pray for more whiskey, then climb under cover and tell old Joe Stalin to go to hell.

10. If you're in the 'Vets' during an Air Raid, stand by the slot machines, that is realy the safest spot in town, they havent been hit for years.

11. If you are hit by a bomb, keep your nerve, dont go to pieces. Just lie still and no one will notice you.

This document is copied as it was written, complete with American spellings, spelling mistakes and grammatical errors.

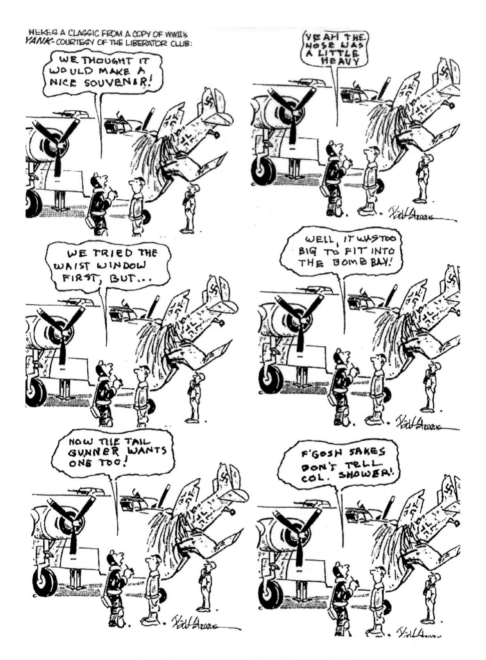

From 'Yank', courtesy of the Liberator Club

CAT HEAVEN

One day a cat dies of natural causes and goes to heaven. There he meets the Lord himself. The Lord says to the cat 'You lived a good life and if there is any way I can make your stay in heaven more comfortable, please let me know.'

The cat thought for a moment and says 'Lord, all my life I have lived with a poor family and had to sleep on a hard wooden floor.' The Lord stops the cat and says 'Say no more' and a wonderful fluffy pillow appears.

A few days later 6 mice are killed in a tragic farming accident and they all go to heaven. Again there is the Lord there to greet them with the same offer. The mice answer 'All our lives we have been chased. We have had to run from cats, dogs, and even women with brooms. Running, running, running, we're tired of running. Do you think we could have roller skates so we don't have to run anymore?' The Lord says 'Say no more' and fits each mouse with beautiful new roller skates.

About a week later the Lord stops to see the cat and finds him snoozing on the pillow. The Lord gently wakes the cat up and asks him 'How are things since you have been here?' The cat stretches and replies 'It is wonderful here. Better than I ever expected. And those "Meals on Wheels" you've been sending by are theeeeeeeee best!

This ditty was found posted around the base.

[108]

Hamm

COMBAT MISSIONS

NO.	DATE	TARGET	NO.	DATE	TARGET
1	Apr. 10, '44	Bourges	43	June 6, '44	Abandoned
2	Apr. 11, '44	Ascherleben	44	June 6, '44	Pontaubault
3	Apr. 12, '44	Recalled	45	June 7, '44	Lisieux
4	Apr. 13, '44	Lechfeld	46	June 8, '44	Pontaubault
5	Apr. 17, '44	Wisernes	47	June 10, '44	Chateaudun
6	Apr. 18, '44	Brandenburg	48	June 11, '44	Blois
7	Apr. 19, '44	Paderborn	49	June 11, '44	Beauvais
8	Apr. 20, '44	Siracourt	50	June 12, '44	Evreux
9	Apr. 21, '44	Recalled	51	June 14, '44	Beauvais
10	Apr. 22, '44	Hamm	52	June 15, '44	Evreux
11	Apr. 24, '44	Leipheim	53	June 17, '44	Guyancourt
12	Apr. 25, '44	Mannheim	54	June 17, '44	Tours
13	Apr. 26, '44	Paderborn	55	June 18, '44	Bremerhausen
14	Apr. 27, '44	Siracourt	56	June 18, '44	Watten
15	Apr. 27, '44	Blainville	57	June 20, '44	St. Martin L'Hortier
16	Apr. 29, '44	Berlin	58	June 20, '44	Ostermoor
17	May 1, '44	Rousseauville	59	June 20, '44	Recalled
18	May 1, '44	Liége	60	June 21, '44	Berlin
19	May 4, '44	Brunswick	61	June 23, '44	Belloy-sur-Somme
20	May 5, '44	Sotterast	62	June 24, '44	Toussus/Paris
21	May 7, '44	Osnabruck			Toussus, Grenoble
22	May 8, '44	Brunswick	63	June 24, '44	Bellecroix
23	May 9, '44	Florennes	64	June 25, '44	Pont-a-Vendin
24	May 10, '44	Diepholz	65	June 25, '44	Bretigny
25	May 11, '44	Epinal	66	June 28, '44	Saarbrucken
26	May 12, '44	Bohlen	67	June 29, '44	Aschersleben
27	May 13, '44	Tutow	68	July 1, '44	Recalled
28	May 19, '44	Brunswick	69	July 2, '44	Pignon Ferme
29	May 20, '44	Rheims	70	July 5, '44	Le Culot
30	May 21, '44	Siracourt	71	July 6, '44	Kiel
31	May 23, '44	Bourges	72	July 7, '44	Lutzkendorf
32	May 24, '44	Melun	73	July 8, '44	Recalled
33	May 25, '44	Mulhouse	74	July 11, '44	Munich
34	May 27, '44	Neunkirchen	75	July 12, '44	Munich
35	May 28, '44	Zeitz	76	July 13, '44	Saarbrucken
36	May 29, '44	Tutow	77	July 16, '44	Saarbrucken
37	May 30, '44	Zwischenahn	78	July 17, '44	Villers/Belloy-sur-
38	May 31, '44	Recalled			Somme
39	June 2, '44	Stella Plage			Haut Maisnel
40	June 3, '44	Berck-sur-mer			Bois de Queue
41	June 5, '44	Bourges			Contesse
42	June 6, '44	Colleville	79	July 18, '44	Troarn

NO.	DATE	TARGET	NO.	DATE	TARGET
80	July 19, '44	Kempton	122	Oct. 19, '44	Mainz
81	July 20, '44	Eisenach	123	Oct. 22, 44	Hamm
82	July 21, '44	Neuaubing	124	Oct. 25, '44	Neumunster
83	July 24, '44	Montreuil	125	Oct. 26, '44	Minden
84	July 25, '44	Montreuil	126	Oct. 30, '44	Harburg
85	July 29, '44	Bremen	127	Nov. 2, '44	Bielefeld
86	July 31, '44	Ludwigshaven	128	Nov. 4, '44	Misburg
87	Aug. 1, '44	Haut Maisnel	129	Nov. 5, '44	Karlsruhe
88	Aug. 2, '44	Remaisnil	130	Nov. 6, '44	Minden
89	Aug. 3, '44	Lille	131	Nov. 9, '44	Metz
90	Aug. 4, '44	Rostock	132	Nov. 10, '44	Hanau
91	Aug. 5, '44	Brunswick/Wagram	133	Nov. 11, '44	Bottorf
92	Aug. 6, '44	Hamburg	134	Nov. 16, '44	Eschweiler
93	Aug. 7, '44	Ghent	135	Nov. 21, '44	Harburg
94	Aug. 8, '44	Clastres	136	Nov. 25, '44	Bingen
95	Aug. 9, '44	Saarbrucken	137	Nov. 27, '44	Offenburg
96	Aug. 11, '44	Strasbourg	138	Nov. 29, '44	Bielefeld
97	Aug. 12, '44	Mourmelon	139	Dec. 2, '44	Bingen
98	Aug. 13, '44	Seine River	140	Dec. 4, '44	Bebra
99	Aug. 14, '44	Dole/Evaux	141	Dec. 6, '44	Bielefeld
100	Aug. 15, '44	Vechta	142	Dec. 10, '44	Bingen
101	Aug. 16, '44	Magdeburg	143	Dec. 11, '44	Hanau
102	Aug. 18, '44	Woippy	144	Dec. 12, '44	Hanau
103	Aug. 24, 44	Misburg	145	Dec. 18, '44	Coblenz
104	Aug. 25, '44	Lübeck	146	Dec. 24, '44	Daun–Gerolstein–
105	Aug. 26, '44	Dulmen			Ober
106	Aug. 27, '44	Recalled	147	Dec. 25, '44	Mechernich–
107	Sept. 1, '44	Recalled			Gerolstein–
108	Sept. 5, '44	Karlsruhe			Hallschlag
109	Sept. 8, '44	Karlsruhe	148	Dec. 26, '44	Niederlahnstein
110	Sept. 9, '44	Mainz, Wurms	149	Dec. 27, '44	Neunkirchen
111	Sept. 10, '44	Ulm	150	Dcc. 28, '44	Neunkirchen
112	Sept. 11, '44	Stendahl	151	Dec. 29, '44	Prum
113	Oct. 3, '44	Gaggenau	152	Dec. 30, '44	Neuwied
114	Oct. 5, '44	Paderborn–	153	Dec. 31, '44	Engers
		Lippstadt–Herford	154	Jan. 1, '45	Guls
115	Oct. 6, '44	Wenzendorf–Stade	155	Jan. 2, '45	Remagen
116	Oct. 7, '44	Magdeburg	156	Jan. 3, '45	Zweibrucken
117	Oct. 9, '44	Coblenz	157	Jan. 5, '45	Cochem
118	Oct. 12, '44	Osnabruck	158	Jan. 7, '45	Rastatt
119	Oct. 14, '44	Cologne	159	Jan. 10, 45	Schönberg
120	Oct. 15, 44	Monheim	160	Jan. 13, '45	Rudesheim
121	Oct. 17, '44	Cologne	161	Jan. 14, '45	Hallendorf

NO.	DATE	TARGET	NO.	DATE	TARGET
162	Jan. 16, '45	Dresden	192	Mar. 12, '45	Swinemünde
163	Jan. 17, '45	Harburg	193	Mar. 14, '45	Giessen
164	Jan. 29, '45	Munster	194	Mar. 15, '45	Zossen
165	Jan. 31. '45	Brunswick	195	Mar. 17, '45	Hanover
166	Feb. 3, '45	Magdeburg	196	Mar. 18, '45	Berlin
167	Feb. 6, '45	Magdeburg	197	Mar. 19, '45	Leipheim
168	Feb. 8, '45	Salzbergen	198	Mar. 20, '45	Hemmingstadt
169	Feb. 9, '45	Magdeburg	199	Mar. 21, '45	Hespe
170	Feb. 11, '45	Dulmen	200	Mar. 22, '45	Kitzingen
171	Feb. 14, '45	Magdeburg	201	Mar. 23, '45	Osnabruck
172	Feb. 15, '45	Magdeburg	202	Mar. 24, '45	Nordham
173	Feb. 16, '45	Osnabruck	203	Mar. 24, '45	Kirtorf
174	Feb. 17, '45	Meschede	204	Mar. 25, '45	Hitzacker
175	Feb. 21, '45	Nürnberg	205	Mar. 30, '45	Wilhelmshaven
176	Feb. 22, '45	Hildesheim	206	Mar. 31, '45	Brunswick
177	Feb. 23, '45	Gera	207	Apr. 4, '45	Perleberg
178	Feb. 24, '45	Bielefeld	208	Apr. 5, '45	Plauen
179	Feb. 25, '45	Schwabisch–Hall	209	Apr. 6, '45	Halle
180	Feb. 26, '45	Eberswalde	210	Apr. 7, '45	Krummel
181	Feb. 27, '45	Halle	211	Apr. 8, '45	Unterschlauersbach
182	Feb. 28, '45	Bielefeld	212	Apr. 9, '45	Lechfeld
183	Mar. 1, '45	lngolstadt	213	Apr. 10, '45	Rechlin/Larz
184	Mar. 2, '45	Magdeburg	214	Apr. 11, '45	Regensburg
185	Mar. 3, '45	Nienburg	215	Apr. 14, '45	Royan
		Bielefeld	216	Apr. 15, '45	Pointe de Grave
186	Mar. 4, '45	Stuttgart	217	Apr. 16, '45	Landshut
187	Mar. 7, '45	Soest	218	Apr. 17, '45	Karlsbad
188	Mar. 8, '45	Dillenburg	219	Apr. 20, '45	Zwiesel
189	Mar. 9, '45	Osnabruck	220	Apr. 21, '45	Salzburg
190	Mar. 10, '45	Arnsberg	221	Apr. 25, '45	Traunstein
191	Mar. 11, '45	Kiel			

CASUALTIES

The following list is from our records at Rackheath and may not be accurate or complete.

CASUALTIES EN ROUTE TO UNITED KINGDOM

On 17th March 1944 one aircraft of the 790th Bomb. Squadron crashed into the Atlas Mountains between Dakar and Marrakech, killing all of the crew:

Mosser, Edward J. 2 Lt	Waterman, Robert P. S/Sgt
Houghton. Earl L. 2 Lt	Detwiler, John K. S/Sgt
Fords Thomas M., Jr 2 Lt	Gorczewski, Anthony J. S/Sgt
Deaves, Robert H. 2 Lt	Green, Gene S. Sgt
Massey, Luther E. T/Sgt	Kelly, Howard J. Cpl

Another crew, ferrying a B-24 for the ATC, crashed on take-off at Dakar, causing casualties and killing four of the crew:

Rubin, Albin M. F/O	Ritchey, Ernest M. Sgt
Bertch, David Sgt	Wallingham, Earl Sgt

KILLED IN LINE OF DUTY IN UK (Practice Missions)

Prewitte, William V. 1 Lt	Aug. 16, 1944	Pendergast, James R. F/O	Jan. 22, 1945
Hall, William H. 2 Lt	Aug. 16, 1944	McArthur, John P. F/O	Jan. 22, 1945
Pattangall, Malcolm N., Jr 2 Lt	Aug. 16, 1944	Stokes, Otto W. F/O	Jan. 22, 1945
Godshalk, George R., Jr 1 Lt	Aug. 16, 1944	Rachword, Clarence J. S/Sgt	Jan. 22, 1945
Grooms, Edward C. 1 Lt	Aug. 16, 1944	Rostkowski, Leonard Sgt	Jan. 22, 1945
Meredith, Oliver E., Jr S/Sgt	Aug. 16, 1944	Erickson, Floyd W. Sgt	Jan. 22, 1945
Dadig, Albert S., Jr Sgt	Aug. 22, 1944	Walker, William E. Sgt	Jan. 22, 1945
Wunrich, Arnold A. F/O	Nov. 9, 1944	Wasson, Frank Sgt	Jan. 22, 1945
Allen, Raymond V. T/Sgt	Nov. 9, 1944	O'Malley, John F., Jr Sgt	Jan. 22, 1945
Ostrander, Lyle M. T/Sgt	Nov. 9, 1944		

OPERATIONAL LOSSES
KILLED IN ACTION

Reed, Russell E. S/Sgt	Apr. 11, 1944	Luna, Paul D. S/Sgt	June 21, 1944
Harahbarger, K. H. S/Sgt	Apr. 11, 1944	Perreault, Joseph V. T/Sgt	June 25, 1944
Eaton, Raymond J. T/Sgt	Apr. 11, 1944	Mikulin, John S/Sgt	July 11, 1944
Dahlin, Axel R. 2 Lt	Apr. 11, 1944	Price, Arthur D. S/Sgt	July 11, 1944
Wilder, Emmett L. 2 Lt	Apr. 11, 1944	Coven, Albert B. S/Sgt	Aug. 3, 1944
Stuckman, Charles L. 2 Lt	Apr. 11, 1944	McCamish, Benjamin F. S/Sgt	Aug. 3, 1944
Skinner, Jack M. 2 Lt	Apr. 11, 1944	Sanderford, Dan M. 2 Lt	Aug. 3, 1944
Williams, Abel J. S/Sgt	Apr. 13, 1944	Collins, Richard J. 2 Lt	Aug. 3, 1944
Caluorai, Ernest 1 Lt	Apr. 13, 1944	Schneider, Norman E. S/Sgt	Aug. 5, 1944
Snook, Oliver W. 2 Lt	Apr. 20, 1944	Doole, Roy J. 2 Lt	Aug. 6, 1944
Orr, Riley E. S/Sgt	Apr. 22, 1944	Lloyd, Howard A. Sgt	Aug. 7, 1944
McGonigle, Charles D. S/Sgt	Apr. 22, 1944	Evancich, Frank G. Sgt	Aug. 7, 1944
Howe, James R. S/Sgt	Apr. 22, 1944	Finger, Samuel S/Sgt	Aug. 7, 1944
Horak, Richard E. S/Sgt	Apr. 22, 1944	Bishop, Carl S. S/Sgt	Aug. 7, 1944
Carter, George E. S/Sgt	Apr. 22, 1944	Wickerham, George B. 2 Lt	Aug. 7, 1944
Violette, Louis J. S/Sgt	Apr. 22, 1944	Rainault, Rodger B. 2 Lt	Aug. 7, 1944
Wilson, Robert E. 2 Lt	Apr. 22, 1944	Schlomowitz, Sol 2 Lt	Aug. 7, 1944
Landis, Wellington E. 2 Lt	Apr. 22, 1944	Chilver, Harold R. 1 Lt	Aug. 7, 1944
Maxey, J. H. 2 Lt	Apr. 22, 1944	Sakrison, Albert E. S/Sgt	Aug. 13, 1944
Roden, James A. 2 Lt	Apr. 22, 1944	Wilkins, William F. S/Sgt	Aug. 13, 1944
Kovalenko, Walter W. T/Sgt	Apr. 22, 1944	Manley, Leo J. Sgt	Aug. 13, 1944
Hope, Edward W. Sgt	Apr. 22, 1944	Burns, Rufus R. 2 Lt	Aug. 13, 1944
Dery, Sylvia L. T/Sgt	Apr. 22, 1944	Snyder, Philip A. S/Sgt	Aug. 18, 1944
Alier, Louis A. 2 Lt	Apr. 22, 1944	Pontius, Darlton W. T/Sgt	Aug. 18, 1944
Ferguson, James G. 2 Lt	Apr. 22, 1944	Lifschitz, George T/Sgt	Aug. 18, 1944
Mason, Warren W. 2 Lt	Apr. 22, 1944	Sherrill, William M. 2 Lt	Aug. 18, 1944
Reid, Stalie C. 1 Lt	Apr. 22, 1944	Worby, Henry J. T/Sgt	Aug. 13, 1944
Williams, Floyd D. S/Sgt	Apr. 29, 1944	Smith, John 2 Lt	Oct. 14, 1944
Peters, Richard C. S/Sgt	Apr. 29, 1944	Woods, Willard T., Jr S/Sgt	Nov. 5, 1944
Hill, LeRoy M. S/Sgt	Apr. 29, 1944	Loberg, Denver Sgt	Dec. 24, 1944
Boucher, James R. S/Sgt	Apr. 29, 1944	Hanks, Weldon M. 2 Lt	Dec. 25, 1944
Dreksler, Edward J. S/Sgt	Apr. 29, 1944	Sefca, Martin, Jr 1 Lt	Dec. 25, 1944
Condon, Edward H. 2 Lt	Apr. 29, 1944	Walinski, Walter Sgt	Dec. 25, 1944
Millinon, George W. 2 Lt	Apr. 29, 1944	Koley, Stanley P. Sgt	Dec. 25, 1944
Hinkebein, Glen L. S/Sgt	Apr. 29, 1944	Morehouse, Roland L. Sgt	Dec. 25, 1944
Sager, Leonard George S/Sgt	Apr. 29, 1944	Onischuk, Alek Sgt	Dec. 25, 1944
Hamilton, George S. S/Sgt	May 8, 1944	Hardick, Peter, Jr S/Sgt	Dec. 25, 1944
Creighton, Richard C. S/Sgt	May 8, 1944	Ellefson, John N. S/Sgt	Dec. 25, 1944
Fitzjarrell, Edmond M. T/Sgt	May 8, 1944	Vaught, Bertie M., Jr Sgt	Dec. 29, 1944
Teague, Eugene J. 2 Lt	May 8, 1944	Close, Duane E. Sgt	Dec. 29, 1944
Harrison, Charles D. 2 Lt	May 8, 1944	Masiak, Robert J. S/Sgt	Dec. 29, 1944
Ludka, Richard J., Jr. 2 Lt	June 21, 1944	Christian, Lewis C. 2 Lt	Dec. 29, 1944

[114]

Foster, David W. 1 Lt	Dec. 29, 1944	Gore, Joseph A. Sgt	Feb. 3, 1944
Ketchel, Dale K. Sgt	Dec. 29, 1944	Cassels, Hugh R. S/Sgt	Mar. 4, 1945
Williams, Robert L. Sgt	Dec. 29, 1944	Ulerick, James E. S/Sgt	Mar. 4, 1945
Materewicz, Edward R. Sgt	Dec. 29, 1944	Rinesmith, John W. S/Sgt	Mar. 4, 1945
Koller, Karl J. Sgt	Dec. 29, 1944	Dick, James A. T/Sgt	Mar. 4, 1945
Ryers, Lewis E. Sgt	Dec. 29, 1944	Grinkiarious, Michael T/Sgt	Mar. 4, 1945
Montick, Albert Sgt	Dec. 29, 1944	Missiras, Theologos F/O	Mar. 4, 1945
Fearon, Joseph F. Sgt	Dec. 29, 1944	Hatkoff, Nathan M. 2 Lt	Mar. 4, 1945
Hagist, Richard S. F/O	Dec. 29, 1944	Mills, George W. 1 Lt	Mar. 4, 1945
Pheneger, Clifford A. F/O	Dec. 29, 1944	Van Tress, Harold P., Jr. 1 Lt	Mar. 18, 1945
Schellhas, Kurt F. 2 Lt	Dec. 29, 1944		

The German Air Force intruder attack on the base on April 22, 1944 resulted in the death of
Miney, Daniel E. Pvt

MISSING IN ACTION

Haines, L. M. S/Sgt	Apr. 13, 1944	Zielinski, E. S/Sgt	July 11, 1944
Moore, B. F. Lt	Apr. 29, 1944	Younkin, L. E. Lt	Aug. 5, 1944
Kilgore, W. T. S/Sgt	Apr. 29, 1944	Kalienko, S. S/Sgt	Aug. 5, 1944
Braunn, W. G. S/Sgt	Apr. 29, 1944	Kells, S. L. Sgt	Aug. 5, 1944
Atley, D. E. Lt	Apr. 29, 1944	Coltey, E. Z. Lt	Aug. 5, 1944
Russell, R. T. S/Sgt	Apr. 29, 1944	Kramer, W. R. Lt	Aug. 5, 1944
Davis, R. C. S/Sgt	May 8, 1944	O'Hara, J. H. S/Sgt	Aug. 5, 1944
Vogel, R. D. S/Sgt	May 8, 1944	Klemas, J. J. S/Sgt	Aug. 5, 1944
Brannan, G. H. S/Sgt	May 8, 1944	Besney, J. M. S/Sgt	Aug. 5, 1944
Stephens, R. B. Lt	May 29, 1944	LeBar, B. C. S/Sgt	Aug. 5, 1944
Peacock, C. T/Sgt	May 29, 1944	Kotraba, G. J. Lt	Aug. 6, 1944
Jenkins, F. C. S/Sgt	May 29, 1944	McCartney, S. A. Lt	Aug. 6, 1944
Walther, G. S/Sgt	May 29, 1944	Kirby, J. W., Jr. F/O	Aug. 6, 1944
Carchietta S/Sgt	May 29, 1944	Gage, D. R. Cpl	Aug. 6, 1944
Helton, E. M. Lt	June 21, 1944	Jez, T. F. Sgt	Aug. 6, 1944
Borchick, F. T/Sgt	June 21, 1944	Corbin, S. R. Sgt	Aug. 6, 1944
Gensert, T. A. S/Sgt	June 21, 1944	Herring, A. I. S/Sgt	Aug. 13, 1944
Brezowski, S. S/Sgt	June 21, 1944	Montgomery, R. E. S/Sgt	Aug. 13, 1944
Margiosso. C. S/Sgt	June 21, 1944	Steinbrenner, S/Sgt	Aug. 13, 1944
Knowles, C. L. S/Sgt	June 21, 1944	Hudson, D. J. Lt	Oct. 14, 1944
Greble, W. E. Lt	June 29, 1944	Ostrander, L. M. T/Sgt	Nov. 9, 1944
Robinson, J. E. Lt	June 29, 1944	Allan, R. V. T/Sgt	Nov. 9, 1944
Van Veen, F. P. S/Sgt	June 29, 1944	Weinrick, A. A. F/O	Nov. 9, 1944
Fisher, R. C. S/Sgt	June 29, 1944	Ungerer, M. M. Lt	Nov. 10, 1944
Murphy, J. J. S/Sgt	June 29, 1944	MacDonald, J. G. Lt	Nov. 10, 1944
Kennedy, J. J. S/Sgt	June 29, 1944	Winebrenner, P. J. Lt	Nov. 10, 1944
Davis, H. P. S/Sgt	June 29, 1944	Young, L. C. S/Sgt	Nov. 10, 1944
Underwood, J. F. Lt	July 11, 1944	McGrath, U. J., Jr. Sgt	Nov. 10, 1944
Gillett, T. R. Lt	July 11, 1944	Quigley, J. Sgt	Nov. 10, 1944

THOUGHTS OF AN AERIAL GUNNER/FLIGHT ENGINEER
8TH AIR FORCE 1944–45
467TH BOMB GROUP (H) 791ST SQUADRON
RACKHEATH. ENGLAND.

Chase the dread of war away,
Tonight we drink and sing to play.
We live this moment, no wish deny,
The war is sleeping, tomorrow we fly.
Peddling back to the bomber's nest,
The fog above could mean a day of rest.
In the early hours, still dark of night,
It's destiny calling at cots flagged white.

These chosen tred a somber beat,
Bombers fueled and men must eat
The airman's mess efficiently feeds
These reluctant birds.
Now fully awake to reality,
Each man his courage regirds.
Their step increases, their voices regained.
Questions of target not yet explained.

The briefing room murmurs like friends at a wake,
Sorry he's gone. But none his place to take.
The silence returns as the briefing officer appears.
A pathetic performer who seldom rates cheers.

Behind the curtain a course is laid down,
A blood red ribbon to some German town.
An eruption of sound as the curtain is drawn,
Some souls here will miss the second dawn.

After the briefing each man his equipment receives.
A soft suit of armor or his blood will freeze,
A mask to give life where there is no air,
Maps, money and candy on the bill of fare.
And then the friend no airman denies,
His silver white chute whenever he flies.

The padre is smiling in the gentle light,
For each man was given his final rite.
These grotesque warriors leave behind
The last quonset hut their bird to find
Squatting in wait like an aging whore,
They have a date with a B-24.

The dark is aging as each silent band
Quietly gathers at their own hardstand.
A check of the craft from nose to fin,
Then all of the creatures vanish within.
Like giant waves striking a rocky shore,
The Liberator motors splutter and roar.
Then they lumber in a menacing gait,
Angry because of the bothering weight.
Like parts of a clock that's gone awry,
The lumbering ducks queue to fly.

With motors full rev and brakes still on,
They shiver and shake and then are gone,
Down the runway they hurriedly flee,
All praying they can outrun gravity.
Motors, wings and skill of hand,
Lift and hold us above the land.
Now slowly rising in circling flight,
Gathering together above the night.

When we are gathered and in formation,
Eastward we sail from this island nation.
The land is ending, it's water ahead.
The Channel's cold water all airman dread.
Over the water all gunners test fire.
To protect his crew is the gunner's desire.
The higher we go the colder it gets,
At sixty below a man still sweats.

The coast of France is on the horizon,
Soon spotty black death with be rising.
The twisting turrets search the clock around,
Approaching bandits give no warning sound.
The sky is empty of enemy gun,
I'm sure all pray for a quiet milk run.
The nearing I.P. means soon we must turn
Steady on the line though your soul they burn.

[117]

No enemy fighter dares the deadly bomb run,
For flak never comes from a friendly gun.
It's guts and honor that holds a plane steady,
For the test of flame the 8th is ready.

The Hun below with his radar so clear,
Steadies his aim as we draw near.
Four black steps the heavens climb,
Black notes without music or rhyme.
Lesser men might have turned away.
These hold true into the fray.
A plane is spinning down like a broken toy,
Let me count ten Lord as chutes deploy.
Place the red white and blue on a dark green wreath,
Some boys will be missing from old Rackheath.

Feel that lift? Like a kite at play,
The bomb runs completed it's bombs away.
No need to fly straight, now we can turn,
Mission accomplished. No need to burn.
The flak is slowing as we make our turn
And the words are flowing. To England return.

The target is burning way down below,
The props steadily turning, a long way to go.
The hour is called, the guns point high,
Jerry is coming, some mothers will cry.
Remember to lead and make the bursts short.
The rounds in the can are all you've got.
Each Jerry takes aim, breaks into the curve.
We hate their guts, but admire their nerve.

The plane off your wing has friends aboard,
Fingers of fire shatter and sever the cord,
Out of control, a sad wounded bird,
Some unknown hunter is thinning the herd.
Follow her down till she's out of sight,
You're praying now, you'll be drinking tonight.
As quickly they came, swiftly they're gone.
So much has happened after the dawn.
Some friends are gone, may never return,
The next time out it could be your turn.

The group has been lowering at a steady pace,
We finally can remove the mask from our face,
Relax a little, make a joke,
Talk a little, sigh or smoke.

We've crossed the Channel once again,
Converted from killers to gentler men.
I thank the Lord for every round trip
And pray He will never desert our ship.

Thanks to the ground pounders all over the base.
The ground pounders lot is a harried pace.
We are the riders, the favorite son,
Without our walkers no task is done.

We've been debriefed, relived the day,
Now set loose to sleep or play.
The drink I had plays havoc with me,
The rhymes in my head hum tauntingly.
Crazy thought fling sounds in my brain.
Many times I've heard this refrain,
"Up around the Zyder Zee
Charlie took a shot at me."

Paul J. Kuchinski

Mission completed

Nose art

The following songs were sung by the men of the 467th. Many more were rewritten to the tune of existing songs.

AFTER THE MISSION'S OVER
(It is thought to the tune of 'After the Ball is over')

After the mission's over,
After we all get back,
We get interrogated,
"Where did you see the flak?
How were those German fighters
When were your bombs away?
Does anyone have any bitches?
That's all for today."

We like the Liberator,
We think it handles well,
We like to fly formation
We're all as nuts as hell.
We like that fighter reel-off
It'll kill us all some day
You land it in thirty seconds
Or AL will have to say –

"Condy, you straggled all day,
Tibbets showed poor technique,
Huston, you had your head up
We'll have a short critque,
You missed the D.A.L., Jones,
Johnson, you will report,
Why you thought that one wing off
Was reason to abort.

F. J. Jansen
E. F. Jenkins

RACKHEATH AGGIES
(Tune unknown)

Rackheath Aggies,
Rackheath Aggies,
Out to do or die

Rackheath Aggies,
Rackheath Aggies,
Fumbling through the sky.

Our formations are sensations,
We're not easily cowed,
We'll drop our bombs
Until those fields are plowed.

Author unknown

PETER THE POM INSPECTOR
(Tune unknown)

From the Nation's capital there came a man
Whose job was rather tough,
He took a look at our fine group,
And said "That's not enough".
So in formation our group did fly,
Bombs were dropped all over the place,
And not a man sick or did die.
But you should have seen the look on the Colonel's face.

But twas nothing compared to the look ooon the face
Of Peter the POM Inspector.

Peter pondered AGO's, dog tags and form fives
He read more poop about this group
Than we could all our lives.
He scrutinized with a practised eye
Our take-off's and formations
To see if we could really fly according to regulations
He interviewed most every flier that he could find, and then
He told the group of his desire to fly with them again.

[122]

So, S-2 briefed the group like mad,
While every crewman dozed.
Then Base called up and said "Too bad
This goddam field is closed".

He would never never lie,
He would very much rather die
A very upstanding guy was he,
Was Peter, the POM Inspector.

So, without hesitation or procrastination
Our group took off once more
With good navigation and co-ordination
They hoped to win the war
With determination this big congregation
Went winging over the blue.
Their fine adaptation to the whole situation
As really something new.

Author unknown

Nose art

Nose art

Nose art